PROFITS, POLITICS AND DRUGS

Also by W. Duncan Reekie

ADVERTISING
THE ECONOMICS OF THE PHARMACEUTICAL INDUSTRY
MANAGERIAL ECONOMICS
MANAGEMENT IN THE SOCIAL AND SAFETY SERVICES (*with N. C. Hunt*)
THE CONSUMER SOCIETY (*with I. R. C. Hirst*)

PROFITS, POLITICS AND DRUGS

W. Duncan Reekie and Michael H. Weber

First published 1979 by
THE MACMILLAN PRESS LTD
London and Basingstoke
Associated companies in Delhi
Dublin Hong Kong Johannesburg Lagos
Melbourne New York Singapore Tokyo

Typeset in Great Britain by
Preface Ltd, Salisbury, Wilts
and printed in Great Britain by
Redwood Burn Limited, Trowbridge & Esher

British Library Cataloguing in Publication Data

Reekie, William Duncan
Profits, politics and drugs.
1. Drug trade
I. Title II. Weber, Michael H.
338.4'7'6151 HD9665.5

ISBN 0-333-24006-5

For Ruth and Grace

Contents

Preface

Walter Bagehot once observed that the theory of business had a life of obstruction because 'theorists do not see the business and men of business will not reason out the theories'. Nowhere is the truth of this observation more amply demonstrated than in the case of the pharmaceutical industry. Much academic study of the industry has been at best impressionistic and at worst misleadingly inaccurate. Political and regulatory control of the industry has ranged from the trivial to the harmful. The industry, for its part, has either ignored the criticisms in the hope that they would cease or has, on occasion, adopted such an aggressively defensive posture that ill-informed critics have simply felt that their views had received confirmation.

In the last decade, however, this position has been changing. Economists with a real comprehension of the realities of commercial life and an awareness of the weaknesses of economic theory have been studying the pharmaceutical industry. Their work has done much to improve our understanding of the competitive process in pharmaceuticals and its implications for social welfare. The following chapters owe much to these earlier writers, both British and American.

This book has two main advantages over earlier work, however. Not only does it present an up-to-date picture of the industry but in addition it presents the results of recent international research by each of the authors. It is not simply a literature review. Second, the authors are respectively an industrial economist, and a marketing research expert with many years practical experience as manager in different multinational drug firms. This blend of authorship we believe will overcome what Bagehot would have called 'obstructions' to a proper understanding of the drug industry. Whether we are correct in this belief will ultimately be judged by the only objective yardstick, the market for this book. The Conclusions are our joint responsibility. Reekie contributed Chapters 1 and 4 to 8, Weber provided Chapters 2 and 3.

W. Duncan Reekie
Michael H. Weber

Acknowledgements

Thanks are due to Mr S. Seltzer of IMS World Publications and to Mr H. Evans of IMS International for their assistance in the evaluation of material. Support was also received from Mr L. E. Uytterelst.

M.H.W.

My gratitude goes to Mr Fred Roll of the University of Rochester Medical School. He reawakened my interest in this fascinating industry.

W.D.R.

1 Whence They Came and What They Do

The international research-based pharmaceutical industry has had a spectacular record of technological achievement and economic growth over the past 30 years. It is hard to remember that in its present form it was virtually non-existent in the 1940s. Up to that time, the manufacturers of medicines were still the lineal descendants of the traditional wholesale chemists and druggists, who had been concerned mainly with the manufacture and sale of galenical medicines derived from naturally occurring animal and vegetable ingredients. Bitter aloes, belladonna, cascara, digitalis, ergot and fennel were still typical raw materials for the tinctures and tablets which were their stock-in-trade. It was only from the late 1940s onwards that the specific active chemical ingredients for a new generation of medicines started to emerge from the industrial pharmaceutical research laboratories. The emergence of this new industry and its products not only had an immense scientific and technological impact on the practice of medicine; the development of the radically new chemotherapeutic products also called for new pharmaceutical marketing techniques.

For the best part of the previous two millenia, pharmacology and therapeutics had been based on the teachings of Galen. There had, of course, been major advances, such as the discovery of digitalis and chloroform, the purification of the alkaloids and the development of vaccination. In addition, from the fifteenth century onwards chemists following the precepts of Paracelsus had started to think in terms of crude synthetic medicinal chemistry. There had even been a few significant developments in this field such as Aspirin, Salvarsan and, in the 1930s, Prontosil and 'M and B 693'. However, in the main all that the traditional manufacturing chemists and druggists had had to promote to doctors until the 1940s had been elegant 'ethical' brands of the traditional galenical preparations. The Eli Lilly catalogue for 1943, for example, still listed fluid extract of dandelion. These ethicals had been presented to potential prescribers with discretion and diffidence, because the druggists' 'travellers' needed to draw a sharp distinction between their own sales efforts to the medical profession and those of the strident market-place hucksters who were at the same time selling branded 'Patent Medicines' to the impressionable nineteenth and early twentieth century public.

But in the late 1940s the medical profession, which had so far experienced only the restrained commercial atmosphere created by the modest sales promotion activities of the small traditional 'ethical galenical houses', was suddenly subjected to the full force of the professional marketing activities of the new large-scale international pharmaceutical manufacturers.

Economists usually define an industry from one of two viewpoints: that of the producer or that of the consumer. From the producer's position, industry boundaries are indicated by the immobility of productive resources. If the same productive resources can be easily used to manufacture two or more distinct products, then the products come from the same industry. From the consumer's position, if two or more products are regarded as acceptable substitutes for one another then they are produced in the same industry.

The pharmaceutical industry as seen by the consumer is the group of firms manufacturing and distributing medicines in finished forms such as ointments capsules, tablets and syrups. The industry as seen by the producer performs the following manufacturing and processing activities:

1. Bulk manufacture of synthetic organic chemicals, such as vitamins, antihistamines, diuretics and sulphonamides. These, often complex, substances include many different classes of drugs.
2. Bulk manufacture by fermentation, synthesis, or both, of antibiotics such as penicillin and streptomycin, which are normally made by the culture of micro-organisms, followed by their extraction and purification.
3. Preparation of sera and vaccines by micro-organism culture and the extraction and purification of the antibodies or antigens which are formed.
4. Production from naturally occurring animal or vegetable sources of drugs such as insulin, hormones and morphines.
5. Processing of bulk drugs into finished forms such as tablets, capsules and ointments.

Both definitions are necessary and are complementary. But this book is concerned with the ethical pharmaceutical industry. Specific restrictions and exclusions will render them more precise and meaningful to the following pages. Products for veterinary use will not be included in the industry's product mix; nor will patent or proprietary medicines. Propriepritary or patent medicines are products available for sale, 'over the counter', to the general public, and are frequently publicly advertised. The remaining products are known as ethical or prescription drugs.

The advertising of ethical drugs is restricted primarily to the medical profession. They are generally available to the public only if supplied by a pharmacist authorised by a doctor's prescription. A further important distinction between ethical and non-ethical or proprietary medicines is that the latter tend to have a low research content and a long product life. Ethical drugs, on the other hand, tend to be relatively short-lived and are usually products of a comparatively high degree of research effort.

ORIGINS AND HISTORY

The saga of pharmacy began when man first applied herbs to relieve pain or dress wounds. From this initial step followed the blending of different herbs with each other or with chemicals, such as mercury or sublimed-sulphur. Between the twelfth and fourteenth centuries the British herbalist was adding drugs and spices of Arabian, and later, South American origin to his collection. These were introduced first by the Crusaders and later by various seafaring merchants. At this time, particularly in London, the grocery trade and the pepperers and spicers often overlapped. Their imports were frequently the same and so the functions of grocer and apothecary were often combined.

The increasing variety of unfamiliar drugs and the wider use of chemicals led to more specific skills being required in manufacture and blending. This made it increasingly difficult to combine the activities of grocer and apothecary and in 1617 the joint London Guild split up and the Society of Apothecaries was formed.

Over the next two centuries a gradual shift of emphasis from pharmacy to medicine occurred in the ranks of the apothecaries. This left a partial vacuum in the supply of drugs which was filled by retailing chemists and druggists. In 1841 the Pharmaceutical Society was formed which embraced the chemists, druggists and the remaining apothecaries with a predominant interest in pharmacy. Figure 1.1 illustrates this development.

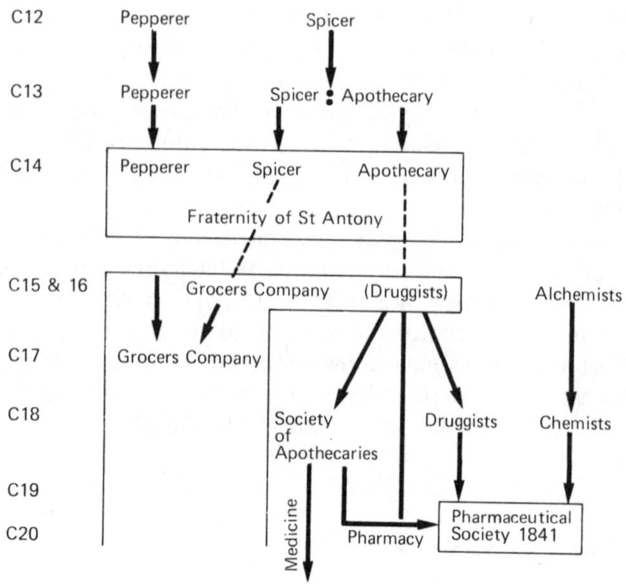

Fig. 1.1. Evolution of the London apothecary and pharmacist.
Source: F. M. L. Poynter, *Evolution of Pharmacy in Britain* (Pitman, 1965).

Many of these chemists and druggists developed into wholesalers and ultimately into manufacturers. Some of today's familiar names in the pharmaceutical industry developed from such origins. For example, the retail chemists and druggists of the nineteenth century, Allen, Hanburys and Barry, is today's Allen and Hanbury Ltd.

Increasing complexity of manufacture was one factor in the trend away from back-shop to factory production. The hand-rolled pill gave way to the compressed tablet. Processes such as varnishing, gilding or silvering pills 'to disguise unpleasant odours or taste . . . were superseded by the introduction of sugar and pearl coatings which were difficult to perform on a dispensing scale with the result that these coated pills, and indeed most pills, passed into the hands of the large-scale manufacturer'.[1]

The most important factor accelerating this trend was the advent of chemotherapy which transferred many of the functions of the pharmacist to the chemist, pharmacologist and clinician. The beginnings of chemotherapy are associated with the name of Paul Ehrlich (1854–1915). Ehrlich built on Robert Koch's observations that certain aniline dyes could kill bacteria. Ehrlich realised that if these dyes could attach themselves to diseased bacteria without harming whole body tissues or cells then he would have made a tremendous contribution to medical science. His search for the 'Magic Bullet', a drug which would seek out its own target, was not short.

Eventually, in 1904, his researches produced salvarsan, a 'Magic Bullet' which kills cellular organisms connected with syphilis.

Despite this promising start, a quarter of a century had to pass before the next major pharmaceutical discovery. Calder has pointed out that before 1935 the physician had only six specific medicines in his armoury; that is, medicines 'capable of attacking causes'. The six were vitamin therapy, quinine, digitalis, ipecacuanha, mercury and salvarsan. 'Only one, Ehrlich's salvarsan, was a truly modern preparation'.[2]

In 1935 what is now called the 'therapeutic revolution' was launched.[3] Dr Gerhard Domagk discovered the antimicrobial qualities of Prontosil, a red dye. A year or two later, in France, it was established that it was an active constituent of the dye, sulphonilamide, which was active therapeutically. Attempts to improve the efficacy of Prontosil resulted in the production of May & Baker Ltd's M & B 693 in 1938.

Penicillin, although discovered by Fleming in 1928, became first available for practical purposes after 1940. Streptomycin, a drug effective against tuberculosis was discovered by Waksman in 1943, and the first of the broad-spectrum antibiotics (chloramphenicol) was introduced in 1949. Tetracycline (1953) was the first antibiotic to be produced where its chemical formula was known prior to the drug itself.[4]

By 1950 the therapeutic revolution was well and truly under way. Corticosteroids, antihistamines, antidepressants, diuretics and many other preparations helping to alleviate human ailments were discovered, developed and are now being produced by the drug industry. Figure 1.2 clearly illustrates the path of the therapeutic revolution. It reflects the spectacular increase in the number of known, important drugs which began with the discovery of Prontosil. Based on pharmaceutical patent activity in London from 1900, it reveals a tremendous upsurge of patenting after 1935. Between then and 1966 exponential growth was present and there was no indication of a reversion to an S-shaped logistic curve. The chemists and druggists who began to manufacture in the nineteenth century had to adopt many new techniques after the chemotherapeutic revolution. Knowledge of technologies associated with chemical processing and dyestuffs expertise and with fermentation was essential. Simultaneously entry

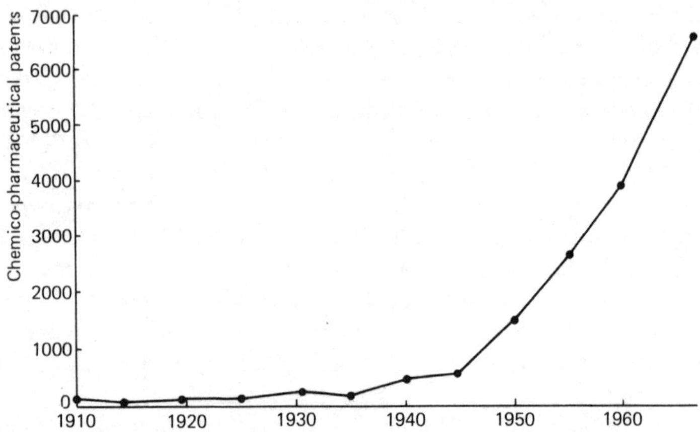

Fig. 1.2. Chemico-pharmaceutical patents in five-yearly periods, 1910–1966. (The 1910 observation is based on ten years preceding data.)

Source: W. D. Reekie, 'Patent Data as a Guide to Industrial Activity', *Research Policy*, 2 (1973) p. 249.

into pharmaceuticals by firms engaged in industries which already utilised these techniques was occurring — for example ICI Dyestuffs Division and Distillers Co. Ltd., respectively. This process of industrial expansion and technological advance was replicated overseas.

In Britain this coincided with an increasing awareness and demand for the benefits of good health, which was formalised by the establishment in 1948 of the National Health Service. The combination resulted in a tremendous expansion in the output of the industry, by existing members, by entrants from other industries and by immigrant subsidiaries bringing with them discoveries and products unique to themselves.

The impact of the world-wide increase in drug discoveries is mirrored in the record of entry by overseas companies into the UK market. The Association of the British Pharmaceutical Industry, whose members supply the NHS with almost all of its drug purchases, has around fifty foreign-owned member companies. Six of these are old-established companies in the UK with dates of entry of 1920 or earlier. A further nine entered between 1920 and 1935. The remainder all entered the British market as subsidiaries subsequent to the discovery of Prontosil in 1935.

These companies did not gain a foothold in the UK market because they attempted to produce existing drugs at a lower price, they succeeded because they were offering newly discovered unique products. This process of discovery and breaking into foreign markets is still going on. Around twenty companies have set up subsidiaries here since 1960, half of them in the last decade alone. Similarly Beecham, a UK firm with a number of major discoveries to its credit, has set up five overseas manufacturing subsidiaries since 1963.

A more comprehensive picture of the impact of the post-1935 wave of discoveries can be obtained from a study of the industry's growth.[5] Over 95 per cent of today's products were unknown in 1950. In the 1920s, some six drugs, either singly or in combination, accounted for over 60 per cent of prescriptions written. Output in Britain rose from a pre-war figure of £21 million to £894 million in 1976, and the US industry from $150 million to world-wide sales of $12,200 million. In 1975 total production in the West amounted to some $43,000 million. Over the past five years alone, the world market has been growing at 14 per cent per annum. In Japan, the market growth rate has been 13 per cent, in Western Germany 14 per cent, in Britain 16 per cent and in the USA 9 per cent.

RECENT TRENDS IN THE INTRODUCTION OF NEW DRUGS

In sharp contrast to the above there is little doubt that the rate of new product introductions in the industry has declined drastically in recent years. According to one analyst in the USA, in 1949 a 'high' of 559 innovations was recorded and a 'low' of 83 in 1969.[6] A more meaningful measure is the number of new chemical entities (NCEs) because they include nearly all major therapeutic advances. (That is, NCEs exclude new combinations of existing products, new dosage forms, or new brand names.) Table 1.1 shows the annual number of NCEs approved by the American Food and Drug Administration (FDA) for 1950–75. The trend is clearly downward despite fluctuations between years.

The OECD has explained this phenomena on two grounds.[7] These could respectively be labelled the research depletion and the declining profitability hypotheses. First, the industry, having successfully introduced treatments for a wide range of diseases, now has to concentrate its research upon the very difficult problems presented by the remaining unconquered diseases. The pathology of tumours and viral diseases, for example, is not fully understood. More importantly, both tumours and viruses act within the cell, not outside as do bacteria, making the discovery of 'Magic Bullets' more difficult. And in other areas there are

Table 1.1. Annual FDA approvals of NCEs (1950–75)

Year	No. of NCEs	Year	No. of NCEs	Year	No. of NCEs
1950	44	1959	76	1968	7
51	55	60	55	69	12
52	40	61	43	70	17
53	73	62	30	71	17
54	60	63	13	72	11
55	57	64	25	73	18
56	52	65	23	74	16
57	73	66	18	75	12
58	45	67	23		

Source: Henry Grabowski, *Drug Regulation and Innovation* (American Enterprise Institute, 1976), p. 18.

difficulties in developing satisfactory models for screening and testing. For example, pathologically in rheumatoid arthritis no animal analogy is available. Second, the world-wide increase in restrictive legislation surrounding the industry since about 1960 has steadily increased in complexity. This has raised the cost of development and resulted in firms being more cautious and selective in their choice of products to bring to market. Which of these two explanations is the more plausible we will discuss at greater length in later chapters.

SOURCES OF NEW DRUGS

The origin of pharmaceutical innovations has been a controversial issue. The US Senate Subcommittee on Antitrust and Monopoly (Kefauver Committee) 'contended that nearly all of the important discoveries in recent years had been derived from research work performed outside the industry and that commercial laboratories were concerned primarily with molecular manipulations of new drugs therapeutically quite similar to drugs already on the market'.[8] The anti-industry view was also put forcibly by Professor Mindel Sheps in his 1960 evidence to the American Public Health Association.[9] He repeatedly claimed that of the 6,000 new products of the preceding 12 years, 50 per cent were 'simply' mixtures of known ingredients, 20 per cent were new brand names for old products and 20 per cent new ways of taking old doses. The industry countered that most of the new drugs that were extensively utilised in 1962 originated in industry laboratories.

These opposing views of the industry's research effort clashed in what Comanor[10] termed the 'battle of the lists' with each combatant's list reflecting a different opinion of what constituted significant drug developments. It is improbable that the lists of discoveries or innovations used by either side in the Senate investigation can be regarded as entirely objective. Since then, however, two studies have been carried out using data sources independent of both the industry and its critics and using data generated for purposes neither of attack nor defence of the industry's research effort.

The first study, by Jerome Schnee, covered the period from 1935 to 1970. His sample of discoveries to 1962 was obtained from a study by the American Medical Association. His list of important discoveries from 1963 to 1970 was mainly based on a survey of 170 physicians at medical schools by an independent journal, *The Medical Letter*. The identification of the sources of the innovations was obtained from scanning medical journal articles and the Paul de Haen *New Product Survey*. The sources of data by individual drug and the attribution of discovery was listed by Schnee. His results are summarised in Table 1.2.

Table 1.2. Schnee's distribution of drug discoveries, selected periods (1935–70) (in percent)

Period of introduction	Source of Innovations		
	Industry	Universities	Other
		Unweighted Distribution	
1935–49	52	34	14
1950–62	69	16	15
1963–70	82	9	9
		Distribution Weighted by Sales	
1935–49	33	66	1
1950–62	82	8	10
1963–70	85	8	7
		Distribution Weighted by Medical Importance	
1935–62	52	37	11

Source: David Schwartzman, *The Expected Return from Pharmaceutical Research* (American Enterprise Institute, 1975) p. 13.

The drug industry was the major source of discovery in each period examined. Even in the earliest period it accounted for over half of all significant new products. By 1965–70 the industry's share had risen to a dominant 82 per cent of all discoveries. If the distribution is weighted by sales in order to gauge the economic importance of industry discoveries the picture for the most recent period is basically unchanged and the role of universities, hospital and research institutions in new drug discovery has dropped sharply since 1950. For the 1935–62 period Schnee was also able to use the ratings of physicians responding to the AMA survey. Weighting the raw data by these ('expert' but subjective) ratings still resulted in the industry being judged the most important source of innovation in that early period.

A recent study by David Schwartzman came to similar conclusions. He restricted his sample to NCEs listed in Paul de Haen's *New Product Survey*. The raw list of NCEs was further refined by Schwartzman. He removed the following items: diagnostic aids, hospital solutions, non-absorbed high-molecular-weight compounds, impure extracts of natural origin, new uses and formulations of previously marketed drugs, new single components included in previously marketed mixtures, new salts and esters of previously marketed drugs, and drugs which were later withdrawn. The Merck Index and the de Haen Non-proprietary Name Index were used to identify the source of each NCE classified as 'industrial' or 'other'. The 'other' category includes not only drugs discovered in academic, government, hospital, and nonprofit laboratories, but also those based on previously known compounds and others whose origin is unknown. Schwartzman's list thus makes assumptions which result in the omission of NCEs which might be regarded as unimportant and awards the credit for any remaining NCEs of unattributable origin to non-industry sources. His estimates

Table 1.3. Distribution of drug discoveries introduced in selected periods (1950–69)

	Percentage distribution by period of introduction		
Source	1950–1969	1960–1969	1950–1969
Industry	86	91	88
Other	14	9	12
	100	100	100

Source: Schwartzman, *op. cit.*, p. 10.

are reproduced in Table 1.3. They show that the industry accounted for 91 per cent of the total number of new drugs introduced in the USA in the 1960s and that its share was slightly smaller in the 1950s. Again, as was also shown in Schnee's work, over the years the industry has become an increasingly important source of new drugs.

THE NATURE OF DRUG RESEARCH

The unwillingness of some critics to accept the importance of the industry's contribution is possibly linked to a reluctance on their part to believe that industrial laboratories provide an environment where really creative work can be pursued which will, in jargon terms, 'advance the frontiers of knowledge'. This belief may have a grain of truth in it. Knowledge *per se* is not a saleable commodity. There is little incentive for a commercial concern to pursue knowledge for its own sake. Only if knowledge can, somehow, be product or process linked and so provide extra revenue or reduce costs will a firm conduct research to gain that knowledge. As a consequence most industrial research (in any industry) is either applied research, rather than basic research, or development. Industrial research and development (R & D) tends to build on the basic advances or discoveries made elsewhere.

In pharmaceutical R & D, however, the industry has consistently had to make leaps over the gaps in theoretical knowledge in order to yield new drugs. This is a major obstacle facing researchers in the industry, the still very limited knowledge which exists concerning the relationship between chemical structure and biological activity. If this knowledge could be increased chemicals could then be synthesised specifically for a particular disease and accurate prediction of the efficacy, toxicity and side-effects of the chemical on the patient would be possible. Because of this lack of a developed base of scientific knowledge of aetiology, pharmaceutical R & D can only rarely use the relatively cheap, deductive or 'rational' research approach. Instead, the relatively costly 'random' approach to research must normally be employed.

New chemicals and organisms must be found, for example, either by synthesis in the laboratory or by the examination of naturally occurring moulds, and soils for organisms not previously known. These compounds are then put through what has become a highly sophisticated network of bio-assay screens. Several species of animal will be used in each screen. The screens will test for any pharmacological activity present in the compound. They will provide information on toxicity, on side-effects, on the effect of one dose of the compound, on the effect of repeated dosages of the compounds, and also on optimum dosage size to maximise efficacy while keeping toxicity within acceptable levels. Several hundred man-hours go into synthesis and first biological testing of one compound.

At this stage no tests have been carried out on men and the results obtained from the animals may well be completely different from those which will be obtained when this stage is reached. 'In our present state of knowledge, prudence requires that man should be considered equivalent to the least favoured species.'[11] This almost certainly means that some potentially valuable drugs have been rejected prior to trial in man and also that some dangerous drugs slip through the screens and go on to clinical trials before rejection. Litchfield points out 'that a number of today's useful drugs (*e.g.*, quinine, digitalis) would never reach a clinical trial in the present-day atmosphere.[12]

If a compound successfully passes through the bio-assay screens it is then submitted to a restricted trial in man, frequently members of the research team itself. Here possible species specificity with regard to man is thrown up. Toxic and pharmacological properties of the compound as indicated by the animal experiments are confirmed or denied and the performance of the drug *vis à vis* its clinical equivalents is demonstrated. After this initial clinical trial the knowledge of the drug to date is passed on to consultants in hospitals and other institutions for full-scale clinical trials.

Clinical trials require the skilful and informed use of the 'double-blind' technique: control groups of patients are placed on existing drugs or placebos while a further group is given the new drug. 'Double-blind' implies that neither the doctor nor the patient knows which group is a control at any one time. This minimises any subjective assessment of results or influencing of results by the clinician's or patient's attitudes. Unfortunately, since human beings vary from time to time and place to place, a laboratory situation with all variables totally isolated is impossible. This is one of the reasons why drugs acclaimed as a success after a clinical trial frequently fail to measure up to initial hopes when administered to a larger population over a longer period of time.

Occurring simultaneously with the later stages of the screening tests, the firm's R & D team must be working on the process of manufacture. Dosage form must also be determined and developed to act as a suitable carrier for the drug itself. It must be ensured that the carrier will take the drug to the site required. The particle size must be appropriate for correct dissolution time. The carrier must be made so that it releases the medicament either slowly or rapidly at the optimum rate. The correct dispersing agent must be chosen. With injection preparations, fluid consistency must be appropriate to avoid needle blockage.

Pharmaceutical R & D is thus a lengthy, complex and costly business. An increase in the supply and application of basic knowledge would of course cheapen and shorten the entire process. At present, roughly one compound in 10,000 which enters the screen ultimately emerges as a drug, the rest being discarded. An increase in the use of the rational approach would enable many such rejections to be made deductively without actual expensive 'suck it and see' experimentation; or even without incurring the effort of chemical synthesis. R & D could then be concentrated primarily on those compounds which were known to possess the qualities of a new medicine.

In the meantime it should be no surprise that most discoveries are made in industrial laboratories. Most R & D explicitly directed towards drug discovery is conducted there. Academic scientists are generally attracted towards research into underlying scientific principles, and not enamoured with the routine evaluation of compounds required by the search for new drugs. Moreover, as Schwartzman[13] has indicated, 'because academic laboratories are concerned with the advances of knowledge within separate disciplines, their staffing is rarely multi-disciplinary, whereas multi-disciplinary staffing is needed in the search for new drugs. The industry recognised early that effective drug discovery research required the organisation and efficient management of teams of scientists drawn from several disciplines.'

THE UNFINISHED TASK

Measuring the benefits produced for society by the industry raises a number of complications beyond the scope of this discussion. The benefits can be social, economic or a mixture of both. They may well be the resultants of costs other than those required to purchase the manufacture of existing drugs or the discovery of new ones. Any attempt to measure the benefits is hampered in two main ways.

Firstly, there is the classic welfare economics situation in that not all the relevant costs and benefits may be apparent in the workings of the market as economists normally see it. Secondly, having identified the benefits, it may be impossible to ascertain what proportion of them results from the pharmaceutical industry's operations.

The all-embracing benefit produced by the industry is the improvement of the health of the community. However, identification of that part of improved health due to the drug industry's operations is almost impossible. Improved health is the result not only of advances in medicines; it is also a consequence of higher standards of hygiene, of nutrition, of increased knowledge in fields such as physiology, of improved surgical techniques and many other factors.

Improved health is usually measured by comparative mortality and/or morbidity statistics. Unfortunately such statistics are not easily convertible into meaningful economic measures. Rare attempts have been made to apply cost-benefit analysis techniques to such statistics. One study by Weisbrod lists the economic losses to society of poor health or, conversely, the economic gains of improved health. These include:

1. Premature death causing the loss of a present or future producer.
2. Loss of production during sickness.
3. Productivity and/or future disease-resistance may be lowered after return to work.
4. Disruption of production of absentee's fellow-workers (due to having to 'fill in' etc.) may mean society's economic loss is greater than the individual's.
5. Economic costs of detection, treatment and rehabilitation of patients.[14]

To obtain an accurate economic assessment of the gains of improved health, such benefits would have to be computed for each individual and subsequently discounted to obtain the present value of the future stream of benefits. The difficulties associated with such a task possibly explain why the problem has been so infrequently approached empirically.

Even were such exercises carried out, it still seems unlikely that the contribution made by any one factor, such as the drug industry, would be able to be assessed. The causes of non-economic benefits would be equally difficult to isolate and such benefits themselves would be non-quantifiable. For example, relief from suffering for the patient's relatives and dependants.

In a few disease areas, however, it is possible to obtain a picture of the welfare contribution of the industry to society. This occurs where the

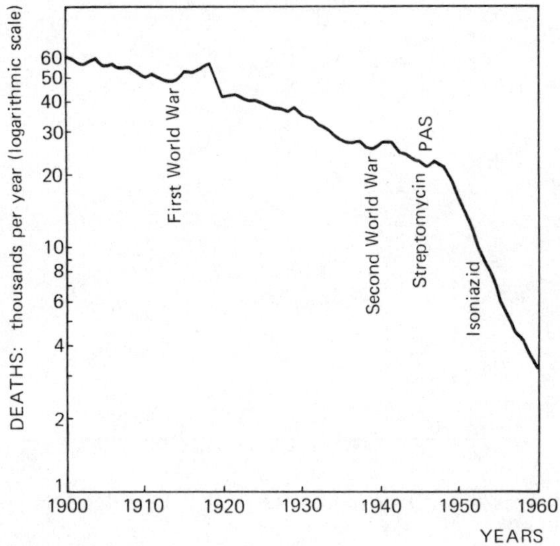

Fig. 1.3. Mortality from tuberculosis. Great Britain (1900–60).
Source: Registrar General.

incidence or killing power of the disease has abruptly declined after a relevant pharmaceutical breakthrough. The decline in mortality from tuberculosis since the introduction of streptomycin, para-aminosalicylic acid, and isoniazid has been one of the most dramatic medical advances of the century (Fig. 1.3).

During the first four years of the National Health Service (NHS) the shortage of beds for tuberculosis patients (and the lengthy waiting lists) was considered a major defect of the NHS. The Ministry of Health had plans for a top-priority building programme for new sanatoriums which failed to materialise only because of a shortage of capital funds. Meanwhile, the pharmaceutical industry discovered, tested, developed, mass-produced, and marketed antituberculosis drugs which swept the whole problem away. In 1953 there was still a great shortage of beds but by 1955 the shortage had gone and ever since increasing numbers of tuberculous beds have been closed (Fig. 1.4). This outstanding social advance was produced neither by the NHS, nor by the Ministry of Health, but by the largely unaided efforts of the pharmaceutical industry.

Another example of the benefits of drugs is child mortality rates. Mortality rates among children in this country have declined

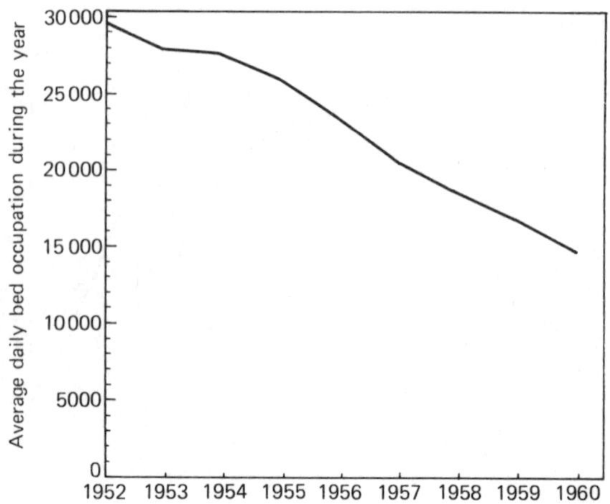

Fig. 1.4. Number of patients in hospital with tuberculosis. England and Wales (1952–60).
Source: Reports of Ministry of Health.

continuously since the mid-nineteenth century (apart from some of the war years when mortality rates were exceptionally high). There are many contributory factors, including public health measures and improved social and economic conditions. In the late 1930s the rate of improvement in mortality rates accelerated rapidly. Coincidental with the change was the introduction of new medicines and vaccines which were capable of preventing or curing many diseases which had hitherto been fatal. One study by the Office of Health Economics (OHE) attempted to quantify the contribution of these revolutionary advances in medicine in preventing premature mortality among children aged 1–14.

The calculation made by the OHE rests on the assumption that, if there had not been this rapid expansion in the effectiveness of medical intervention in the natural history of diseases, then mortality rates in the last thirty years would only have declined at the same rate as they had done between 1901 and 1935. Figure 1.5 illustrates the disparity between actual mortality rates over the past thirty years and projected mortality rates on the basis of the 1901–35 trend. The shaded area represents what may be considered as 'lives saved' by the accelerated reduction in mortality.

In 1968 the total number of deaths among 1–14-year-olds was 496 per million living, or 5235 in absolute numbers. Projected deaths on the

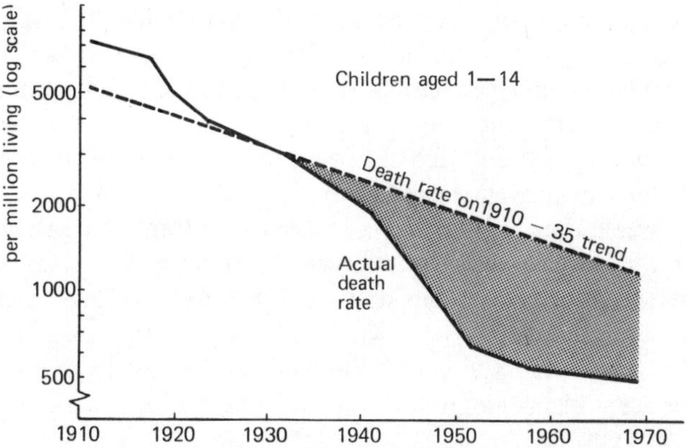

Fig. 1.5. Death rate per million living. England and Wales 1911/15–1968. Five-yearly averages 1911/15–1961/5; annual rates 1966–68.
Source: Office of Health Economics.

1901–35 trend would have been 1207 per million living, or 12,750 in absolute numbers. Thus in 1968 there were 7500 less childhood deaths than there would otherwise have been. Over half of the improvement can be attributed to the near eradication of deaths from five diseases: pneumonia, tuberculosis, diphtheria, measles and whooping cough. In 1931–35 these were responsible for a total of 1570 deaths a year among every million children living. In 1968 this total had been reduced to 51 per million living, of which 46 were due to pneumonia. By comparing actual with projected mortality rates, an estimate can be made of the total number of lives saved since 1935. There were in total about 227,000 persons alive in 1968 who would have died in childhood had the abrupt change in the rate of decline of mortality rates not taken place.

The discovery of the first of the tranquillisers in 1952 and of the anti-depressants in 1960 led to the commencement of psychopharmacology. The use of psychotherapeutic drugs was a major cause, in 1956, of the first-ever annual decrease in the number of occupied hospital beds due to mental illness. From 151,000 in-patients in 1956, the mental-illness hospital population fell to 125,000 in 1966 and less than 100,000 in 1974.[15]

Decreased use of mental-hospital beds was paralleled in other diseases. Improving drug therapy enabled the general practitioner to assume functions previously undertaken by the hospital consultant. For example, Taylor, as early as 1954, said that 'today the practitioner in the gloomiest slum practice can treat pneumonia more effectively than the most eminent specialist was able to do before the war.'[16] This statement is now true of many diseases. Since GP treatment is considerably cheaper per patient than is residence in hospital, this is a further important benefit produced by the industry. (A prescription costs on average, about 129p in total, including chemists' remuneration. If this can prevent hospitalisation, it will mean a saving of over £160 per week, the cost for one patient in the average general hospital.)

Despite these dramatic benefits which the advent of chemotherapy has provided the proportion of total NHS expenditure on pharmaceutical services has as is shown in Chapter 4, Table 4.1, remained virtually static over the years. Since 1973 the steady proportion of 10–11 per cent has begun to fall, and as Table 4.1 indicates is now down to 8–9 per cent.

Table 1.4 places this aggregate information in the perspective of changes in costs of selected health care services. Between 1960–61 and 1973–74 the average cost per in-patient case in acute hospitals with over 100 beds increased 2¾ times, even though the average length of stay had declined and now stands at approximately 9.5 days. Outpatient

Table 1.4. Costs of selected medical services. England and Wales 1960–61 and 1973–74

	1960–61	1973–74	% Increase 1960–1 to 1973–4
In-patients			
Net cost per inpatient case	£53.53	£145.56	172
Outpatients			
Net total cost of each attendance	£ 1.00	£ 4.21	321
Net total cost per new outpatient	£ 3.03	£ 10.92	260
Prescriptions			
Total cost	£83,128,000	£293,500,000	
Average cost per prescription	£ 0.41	£ 0.99	141
General medical services			
Total cost	£90,000,000	£199,367,000	
Average cost per consultation	–	£ 1.36	
Pathological investigations			
Average cost per inpatient week	£ 0.86	£ 3.53	310
Diagnostic X-ray			
Average cost per inpatient week	£ 0.55	£ 1.62	195

Source: Office of Health Economics (OHE), Information Sheet, No. 28, 1976

treatment had also become more expensive: the cost of each attendance had quadrupled and the costs per new outpatient had risen by more than 3½ times. Pathological investigations and X-rays became four and three times respectively as expensive as in 1961. The smallest of the increases during the period has been in the cost of prescriptions (less than 2½ times). On the basis of these statistics the overall average cost of a visit to the doctor, who writes an average of about two prescriptions per consultation, was less than £3.50 in 1974.

Yet despite these achievements, which are impressive in both absolute and in cost-effective terms, there are still many categories of illness where pharmaceutical R & D may still have a large potential contribution to make. No drug yet known can do other than treat the symptoms of rheumatism and arthritis. Yet this is one of the most widespread forms of complaint in all developed countries. In Britain alone 37 million working days were lost due to the disease in 1970–71 and Harris[17] reported that well over one million people have rheumatic conditions which cause them significant physical impairment.

Other areas could be readily cited. Cardiovascular diseases and mental illnesses have been subject to major pharmacological breakthroughs in the past 30 years but much remains to be done. Cancers of various kinds remain untreatable and viral infections have no effective medical remedy.

2 World Markets

Sales of ethical or prescription bound pharmaceuticals are estimated to have reached $40,210 millions world-wide (excluding the Republic of China) in 1976, based on ex-manufacturer price-levels (Fig. 2.1).

Although slow growth was experienced in the early 1970s in most world markets, an acceleration has taken place in the past two to three years which has boosted the average annual compound growth for world ethical sales to 13–14 per cent for the period 1968–76.

CONSUMPTION BY REGION

World consumption patterns are dominated by the countries of the developed world, which in 1976 accounted for around 78 per cent of world consumption of drugs by value.

The Third World markets, perhaps for the first time since 1968, have reversed the 1968–72 trend which showed them accounting for a progressively smaller share of world markets by value (Table 2.1).

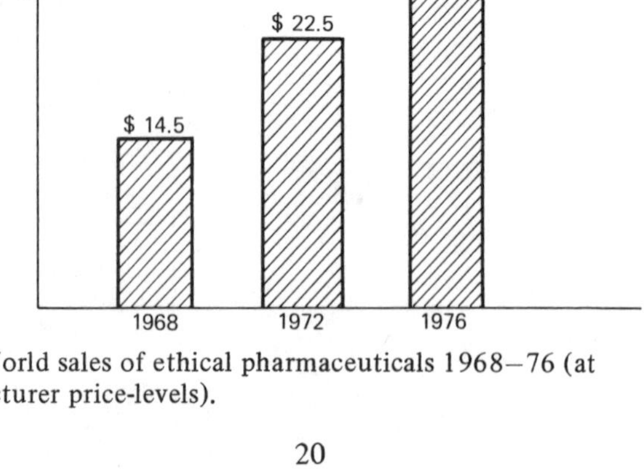

Fig. 2.1. World sales of ethical pharmaceuticals 1968–76 (at ex-manufacturer price-levels).

Table 2.1. Percentage share of the world market in ethical pharmaceuticals by value (1968–76)

	1968 %	1972 %	1976 %
Developed countries	80.1	82.2	77.9
Developing countries	19.9	17.8	22.1
	100.0	100.0	100.0

On a regional basis the most interesting feature of this analysis has been the progressive decline since 1968 of the North American market in world market terms, counter-balanced by an upsurge in consumption in both East and West Europe during the period 1968–76 (Fig. 2.2).

East and West Europe together accounted for just under 50 per cent of world sales in 1976. Whilst reasons for this growth are speculative, one of the most significant factors concerned has undoubtedly been the massive drive by the COMECON countries, not only to become largely self-sufficient in pharmaceuticals, but to become a major exporting force outside the eastern trading bloc. In achieving both these objectives the COMECON countries have not only brought the benefits of chemotherapy to a much wider internal population, they have also

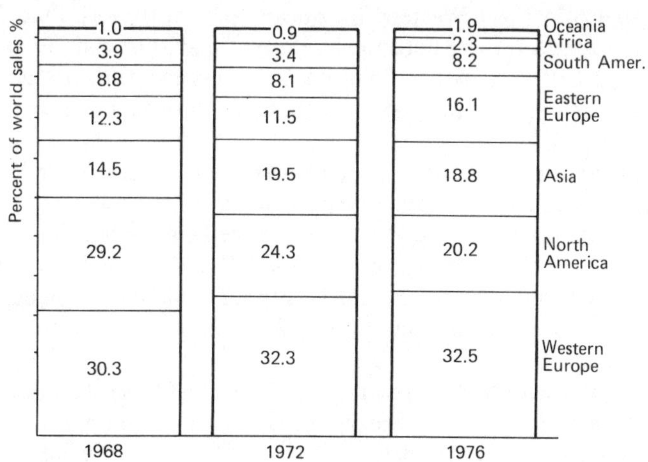

Fig. 2.2. Sales of ethical pharmaceuticals by value on a regional basis (1968–76).

seriously weakened the multi-nationals in many of the countries of the Third World where they have achieved considerable success in marketing their limited range of products.

Three countries in particular, Poland, Hungary and Czechoslovakia, have achieved spectacular production and export growth over the past decade.

Czechoslovakia now exports over 50 per cent of production to around 80 countries world-wide and western countries are the prime targets as far as the higher value added products are concerned. In 1975 SPOFA, the Czech agency responsible for exports, marketed 13 per cent of production to West Germany, 6 per cent to the UK, and overall the 'Capitalist' countries accounted for 52 per cent of production. Poland exports 35 per cent of production currently and is the largest COMECON exporter in cash terms. Reportedly Poland has increased production facilities for ethical products tenfold in the past decade. So far the largest market for Polish products has been the USSR, but the USA and Switzerland have become growing importers of Polish raw materials, particularly opium alkaloids.

Hungary is probably the largest of the COMECON producers and exports around 70 per cent of production by value. Although two-thirds of trade is with the COMECON countries the Hungarian industry is beginning to look outside for lucrative markets in the West. The USSR does not figure largely in world export markets; although around 2000 specialities are produced (compared to an average of 8000–10,000 in most Western European countries) more than 70 per cent of prescriptions are made up by the pharmacist from a standard list of around 250 ingredients. Thus capital investment in production is comparatively low and USSR is thought to be a net importer of pharmaceuticals.

Parallel with the growth of the COMECON countries, the Western European markets have experienced a buoyant growth since 1968. With the growth in Europe of socialised medicine, albeit through the expansion of the Health Care Insurance Funds, the potential of this region is beginning to be realised — although this should be balanced against increasing stringency in pricing which may reduce the growth somewhat.

Africa as a whole has slipped from a 3.9 per cent world market share to a current 1976 figure of around 2.3 per cent. Comparatively, the African markets are extremely poor both collectively and individually. For example, if sales to South Africa are excluded from the African consumption figures in 1976 then sales to the entire African continent

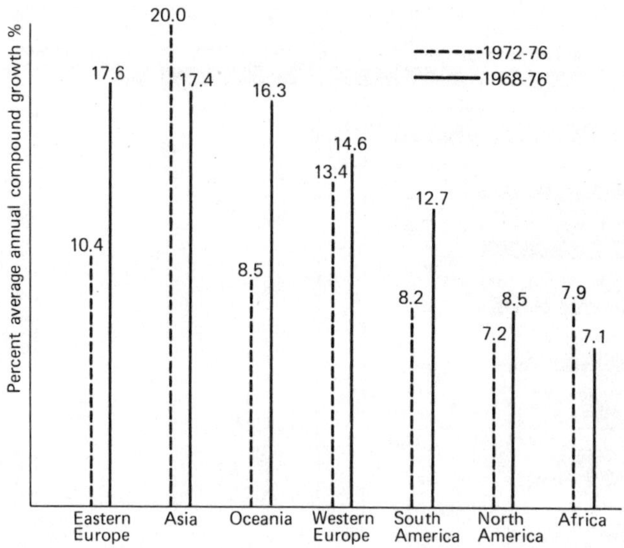

Fig. 2.3. Average annual compound growth rates by region (1968–76).

amounted to only around $640 millions — less than two-thirds the value of the UK pharmaceutical market in 1976.

Asia is dominated by the Japanese market which in 1976 accounted for just under 70 per cent of the sales value for the continent as a whole.

REGIONAL GROWTH

Overall world market growth since 1968 has averaged around 13.5 per cent per annum compound. A few regions, namely Eastern Europe, Asia, Oceania and Western Europe have out-performed this figure, primarily due to the strong growth experienced by the individual countries which dominate each region. Only the North American and African markets have failed to keep pace with this buoyant growth pattern, and even South America has begun to catch up on the more developed regions in growth terms (Fig. 2.3).

LEADING CONSUMING COUNTRIES

Of the 94 countries under study in 1976 the USA is the largest single pharmaceutical market, followed by Japan and the USSR.

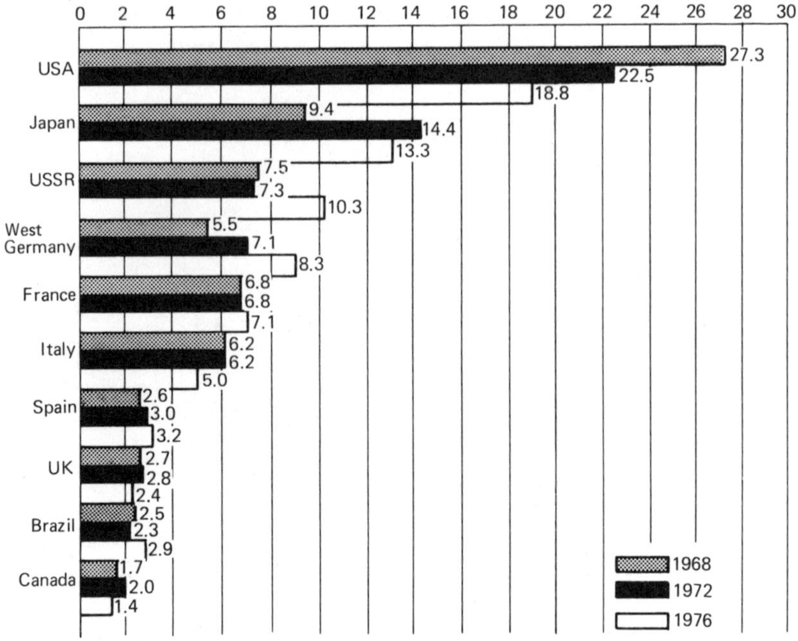

Fig. 2.4. World market shares of leading ten markets by value (1968–75).

The concentration within the leading ten markets is such that around three-quarters of world market value is accounted for by only ten countries — a factor which has remained almost constant since 1968 (Fig. 2.4).

However, in terms of world market shares by value considerable movement has taken place during the 1968–76 period:

1. USA has fallen from a 27 per cent share in 1968 to around 19 per cent currently.
2. Japan has increased its world market share to around 14 per cent from 9 per cent in 1968.
3. USSR has moved from an 8 per cent share to 10 per cent in 1976.
4. West Germany has increased its share of world market sales from 6 per cent to 8 per cent during 1968–76.

On a Regional basis, the dominance exhibited by these major consumers against a world consumption background becomes even more pronounced.

North America — Valued at around $8130 or just over 20 per cent of world sales, this region is dominated by sales in the US market, which in 1976 accounted for around 93 per cent of the region's total sales:

	% Regional sales
USA	92.9
Others	7.1

South America — A number of smallish markets make up the regional total of just under $3300 and the region is dominated by the Brazilian market:

	% Regional sales
Brazil	36.4
Others	63.6

Western Europe — Despite a more even spread in terms of regional shares, three major country markets accounted for around two-thirds of the region's sales:

	% Regional sales
W. Germany	25.7
France	22.0
Italy	15.3
Others	38.0

Asia — Valued at around $7600 millions in 1976 the Asian market consists of four sub-markets:

Western Asia, dominated by Iran
Central Asia, dominated by India
South East Asia, dominated by Indonesia
Eastern Asia, dominated by Japan

Overall the four sub-regions are dwarfed by the Japanese market which in 1976 accounted for around 70 per cent of regional sales.

Africa — Although more of the African countries appear on the league table of leading countries, the region is dominated by three moderately sized markets, South Africa, Egypt and Nigeria, which between them accounted for around 55 per cent of the continent's sales in 1976.

LEADING THERAPEUTIC CLASSES

Analysed purely on a value basis, the leading five therapeutic groups of drugs are estimated to account for 35–40 per cent of the world sales of ethical products (Fig. 2.5).

Antibiotics and Antibacterials occupy a leading position world-wide with an estimated share of 12–15 per cent of world value accounted for by this large group of products. Although much of the impetus for growth in recent years has stemmed from the higher-priced more-sophisticated antibiotics, *e.g.*, the Cephalosporins, there is also a considerable groundwell growth in the simpler, more basic penicillin G and V products which, together with the tetracylines, are probably the most widely prescribed products worldwide.

Sulphonamides have made a considerable comeback in both developed and developing countries due to discoveries of compounds which have considerably enhanced the efficacy of the sulphonamide itself. Undoubtedly as the health care standards of the Third World countries rise, the position of the antibiotics and antibacterials will be enhanced, as these products occupy a key position in the therapeutic armoury of drugs which can be used with the minimum of diagnostic skills — a prerequisite for usage in the developing areas.

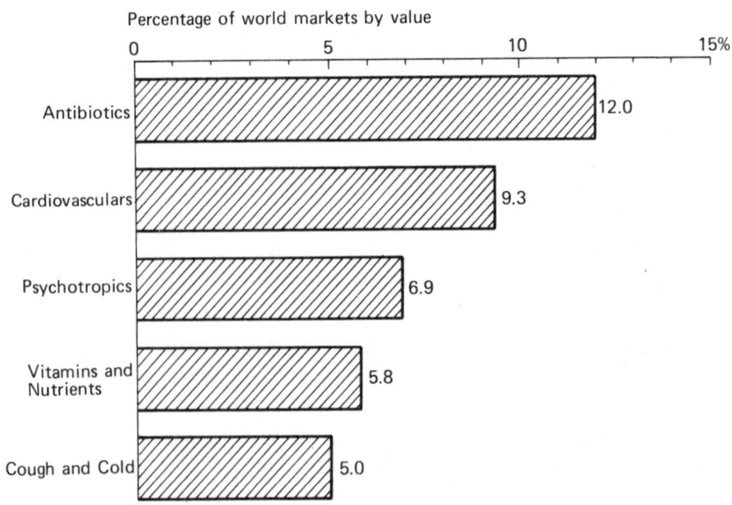

Fig. 2.5. Leading five therapeutic classes worldwide (1976).

Cardiovascular products accounted for around 9 per cent of world consumption of drugs by value. The key in the growth of this class is undoubtedly the growing problems of cardiac disease in the developed countries, coupled with the reasonably high cost of chemotherapy using drugs which are highly innovative and which hence carry a high value added component. The other key influence on growth in this area is that unlike antibiotic therapy, which is largely used in acute illness rarely lasting beyond five days at one time, cardiac therapy is chronic, which means that once a patient is stabilised on a cardiovascular, that product usually forms part of a daily intake for that patient for life.

Stress therapy is becoming more specialised as greater research effort is placed on the underlying reasons for stress diseases such as depression and anxiety. Although primarily a developed-country disease, growth is also being seen within this area in the developing countries as more-sophisticated living patterns are attained. The availability of reasonably inexpensive drug therapy, without the side-effects and problems associated with barbiturates, has led to tremendous advances in outpatient therapy which has alleviated over-burdened and often ineffective in-patient facilities. Undoubtedly the success story of this class in the sixties and seventies has been epitomised by the diazepines (Valium, Librium), products which have allowed patients to be treated whilst going about their everyday activities, and which must have allowed, if measured in purely economic terms, governments to recoup the cost of treatment through having patients carry on their economic activities rather than being in institutions or otherwise incapacitated for work. Psychotropic drugs have made many of the stress conditions generated by the pace of life in the sixties and seventies bearable for a very large segment of the developing world's population.

Vitamins and nutrients owe their strong position as much to the growth of what could be described as 'nutritional illiteracy' in the developed countries, as to the increasing awareness in the Third World of their dietary deficiencies and disease patterns in which deficiency plays a significant role. In addition of course to purely ethical usage, there is a considerable over-the-counter trade in most countries, which is not controlled by prescription and which might double the ethical values calculated for this class of product.

These figures on therapeutic usage however are subject to major caveats. Antibiotics and antibacterials are not normally regarded as being expensive products in terms of daily dosage costs, although it must be said that the more sophisticated hospital antibiotics can be extremely costly. The figures discussed have been computed by value alone, and in some areas, namely cardiovascular and psychotiopics, some products command premium prices, and this tends to distort the comparability of the values shown. Hence the relativities demonstrated between classes may not bear any relationship to the unit usage which is a far more significant (but virtually impossible to obtain) basis for comparison between therapeutic classes. Even more desirable in a comparison of this type would be a comparison of total patient days on each of the therapeutic areas, as this would indicate real frequency of usage.

Another problem which arises in comparing therapeutic class values lies in the definition of the morbidity patterns for which the products within the class are used. As has been mentioned earlier in the text antibiotics tend to be used in acute illness perhaps lasting only five days, whereas products such as cardiovasculars may be prescribed for years on end, with no seasonal fluctuation in demand.

The third key factor affecting the comparability of data lies in the differences which arise between the prices paid for the same drugs by private, government and institutional sectors. The pharmacy, which mainly services the private sector in Europe, must purchase in small packs which decreases the possibility of bulk discounts, a problem exacerbated by the lack of storage space and problems of cash flow associated with maintaining reasonable incentive levels necessary to take advantage of 'special' offers. Government and the institutions, moreover, may forward-buy for up to twelve months in advance, often putting requirements out to tender, and obtaining massive discounts on normal price levels, because of the volume of their business. Where comparisons of value alone are made, therefore, care must be exercised to differentiate between the purchasing bodies, and to assign weightings when assessing the volume of business accounted for by each sector.

DEMAND DEVELOPMENT DETERMINANTS

There are five closely related factors (key indicators) which more often than not determine the rate and character of demand for pharmaceuticals on an individual country basis:

1. Demography – population size, age structure, growth and dispersal.
2. Morbidity patterns – frequency of occurrence of conditions susceptible to chemotherapy.

3. Health care facilities – provision and coverage of the population by adequate 'in' and 'out' patient resources.
4. Health care expectations – personal and group health care norms.
5. Propensity to purchase – availability of government, insurance funds or private resources to purchase health care products.

1. Demography

The anomalies between regions in the consumption of pharmaceuticals are such that in 1976 the developing countries, with around two-thirds of the world's population, accounted for less than one-quarter of the world's pharmaceutical market by value (Fig. 2.6).

In *per capita* terms the implications of such value comparisons are that in 1976 in the developed world *per capita* consumption of ethical pharmaceuticals amounted to \$30.7 whereas comparable figures for the developing countries was in the region of \$5. On an individual-country basis a developing nation such as Pakistan may spend as little as \$1.4 *per capita*, whereas in France the *per capita* expenditure in 1976 exceeded \$50.

However such figures do not necessarily reflect the real differences which exist with regard to health care in the developed and developing countries. For example, whilst the main morbidity pattern in Pakistan is one of conditions susceptible to treatment by relatively inexpensive antibiotic therapy, the morbidity patterns of the more-developed nations such as France are expensive (cardiovasculars, hypnotics and sedatives); and such conditions tend to be chronic, as opposed to the acute patterns of infectious disease. In other words, the probability is high that the quality of health care in the developing countries, based purely on an assessment of *per capita* expenditure, is very poor. However on closer examination the possibility exists that because of

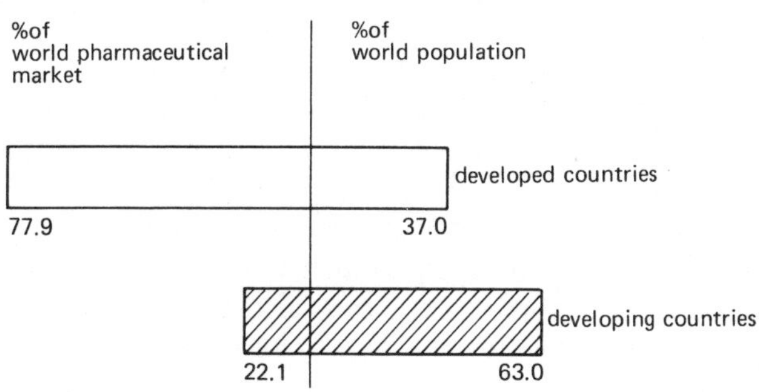

Fig. 2.6. Developed vs. developing world.

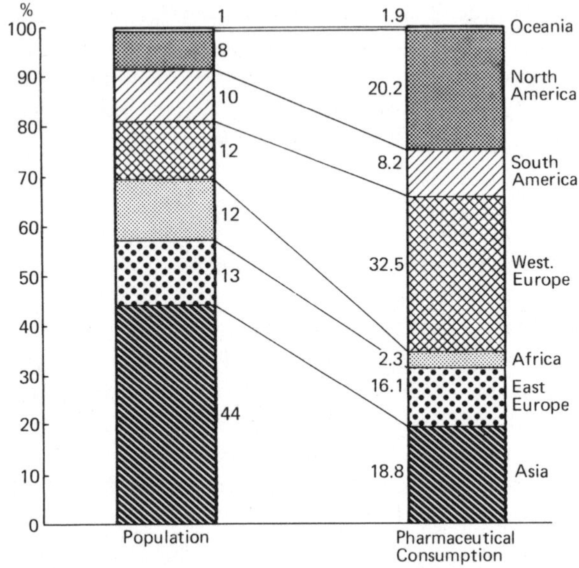

Fig. 2.7. World consumption by region vs. population (1976).

differing morbidity patterns in developing/developed countries, the drugs required are completely different, and those in the case of developing countries are normally considerably cheaper per patient day than the products used for stress conditions in the developed countries. However, whilst the figures may over-emphasise the differences which exist between developed and developing countries there is no doubt that a considerable gap does exist, a gap which is delineated by comparing population and consumption on a regional basis. (Fig. 2.7).

Asia, which has just under one-half of the world's population, accounted for less than one-fifth of the value of the world drug market — and even this figure is misleading as Japan, which accounts for only 4 per cent of the world's population consumed around 13.3 per cent of consumption by value. Rejigging the Asian data to exclude Japan, means that 40 per cent of the world population represented by Asia accounted for only 5.5 per cent of world pharmaceutical consumption by value. Thus in terms of expenditure alone Asia (excluding Japan) must mark as the most underdeveloped region in terms of pharmaceutical consumption — even behind Africa.

On a regional *per capita* basis the real differences between developed and developing nations emerge more clearly (Fig. 2.8). Whilst these

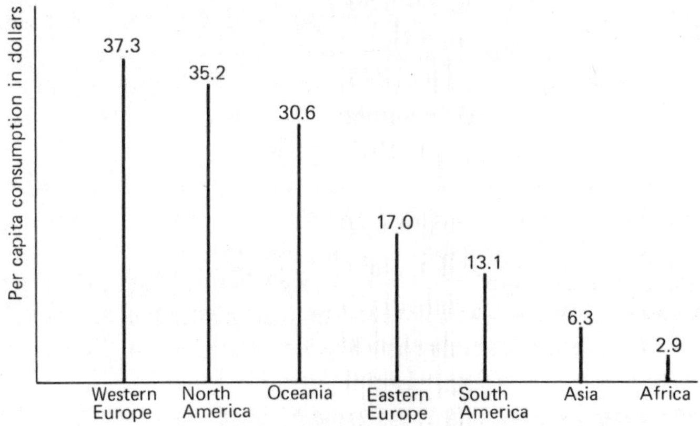

Fig. 2.8. Per capita consumption by region (1976).

figures serve to highlight regional differences in consumption levels it is necessary to make a more effective definition of demographic conditions determining growth in the developing/developed countries.

Population growth in most of the developing nations is well above the 1.6 per cent growth *per annum* figure determined as 'ideal' by the UN. In Asia, for example (the poorest region for pharmaceutical consumption *per capita* if Japan is excluded), many countries exceed this annual average growth by a wide margin (Table 2.2).

Governments have attempted to stem the tide of increasing birth rates by a variety of means:

India resorted to high-pressure sterilisation campaigns, and it was claimed that the programme which started in April 1976 and ran for five months achieved around 2 million vasectomies. Problems arose however over methods used to recruit 'volunteers' and the programme

Table 2.2. Population growth rates for selected Asian countries (1975)

	% Growth per year
Burma	2.4
India	2.4
Indonesia	2.6
Malaysia	2.9
Pakistan	3.1
Philippines	3.3
Thailand	3.3

has now been dropped by the incoming Indian government which has switched to other less controversial methods of birth control.

Indonesia's main problem lies in its culture where girls marry young, and fairly large families of four or five are considered the norm. At current rates of expansion the Indonesian population will double in 35 years, and in order to reduce the rate of expansion the government have embarked on a vigorous campaign of birth control.

Many developing countries' programmes are funded by multinational organisations. The UN through the UN Fund for Population Activities (UNFPA) has an annual budget in excess of $240 million and since its inception has supported more than 1200 projects in over 100 countries.

Obviously one of the major methods of birth control involves the use of oral contraceptives (OC), and already a degree of cooperation exists between WHO and the industry, with the former allowing commercial OC producers access to its clinical testing facilities in return for public-sector rights over sales of the company's OC products in the developing world. However, despite these levels of cooperation WHO itself has commented on the lack of real financial incentives for the producers of OC's — which probably explains the reliance of the industry on dosage permutations for new product introductions rather than carrying out basic research.

The problem remains that the poorer people become, the greater is the risk to health and the incidence of illness. One of the key factors in this chain is the size of family — reduce the population growth in the developing countries and the reduction in pressure on food and land resources will ease the lot of the population. Unless this is done quickly the level of disease in these countries will rise and with it the demand for health care facilities which are already stretched to breaking point. The real problem is that cash for health care is slow to materialise and has often a low priority compared to more tangible items in the industrial infrastructure.

Given present levels of population growth and increases in input levels into the health care system, it is almost inevitable that the current low standards will continue to decline.

Age structure of the developing countries is gradually shifting towards the pattern of longevity of life exhibited in developed societies, and the problems of geriatric populations coupled with a lower incidence in infant mortality rates are beginning to impose themselves. In many cases the developing countries' populations, already grossly outstraining resources of health care and nutrition, will double in two or three decades, given current growth rates coupled with increases in life expectancy (Table 2.3).

The real problems will arise in attempting to serve with health care, the growing proportion of non-productive population, *e.g.*, in India 42 per cent of the population is under 15 years old. The problems associated with an ageing population are also thorny — it is not that this sector consumes proportionally a larger share of the country's drugs bill, but that they are heavy users of in-patient hospital facilities and pressure to expand hospital bed numbers may well lead to a diversion of cash away from pharmaceuticals.

Table 2.3. Population factors for selected Asian countries (1975)

Countries	Birth rate per 1000	Death rate per 1000	Life expectancy	Yrs. till pop. doubles
Burma	39.5	15.8	50	29
India	39.9	15.7	50	29
Indonesia	42.9	16.9	48	27
Pakistan	47.4	16.5	50	22
Philippines	43.8	10.5	58	21
Thailand	43.4	10.8	58	21

By 1985 there is a strong probability that the movement of population from rural to urban areas will accelerate. Whilst this will help the health care problem by bringing more of the population within the ambit of medical facilities, it is likely to create a major problem of pressure on these facilities. Obviously in the depending countries few facilities exist in rural areas for the vast bulk of the population and for the small groups who live in and around the larger villages only rudimentary facilities exist. The movement to the towns will increase the already crowded living conditions in these areas without the basics of sanitation or running water, which will in itself create breeding grounds for communicable disease.

Although many of the developing countries (and WHO) are attacking the major problem of bringing medical facilities to the outlying areas, the problems of the '80s may well lie in another direction, as rural depopulation gets under way and urban centres become overburdened with migrant populations.

As far as the demography of developed countries is concerned, three key issues exist:

1. The projected population growth in the developed countries is in many cases falling below 1 per cent as families decrease under pressure from birth-control programmes, increased female employment, etc. This in itself will create a switch away from the provision of paediatric facilities towards general and geriatric medical care.
2. The movement will be coupled with an increase in life expectancy which by 1990 may reach 75 in the developed nations. Whilst this will increase the scope for geriatric services it does mean, taken together with the shift away from a younger population bulge, that the ratio of productive to unproductive workers may well prove too unbalanced and that the shift towards geriatric care may well remove resources allocated to chemotherapy.
3. Even in the developed nations urban populations are still growing faster than rural — and this concentration is placing increasing strain on the already overburdened urban health care facilities, to say nothing of the increase in stress disease.

2. Morbidity patterns

It could be predicted that overall morbidity patterns are reflected in the demand for certain categories of chemotherapy. Certainly if this is to be accepted then the world-wide pattern of disease in 1976 in order of importance must rank as follows:

1. Infections susceptible to antibiotics.
2. Cardiac complaints.
3. Anxiety and depressive illness.
4. Dietetic and nutritional deficiencies.
5. Coughs and colds.

However, this is over-simplifying the problem, and this approach highlights only those conditions which were treated using chemotherapy. It ignores both the vast mass of untreated illnesses which can only be guessed at within the general populace, and also those consultations where a diagnosis is made but no drug is given. Additionally, the differences that exist at regional level are considerable. The developed nations tend to spend more on the treatment of symptomatic disease patterns, whereas in the developing world the main thrust is against major endemic diseases such as malaria, and eradication programmes of considerable size in terms of expenditure are carried out each year.

Together with immunisation programmes on such diseases as measles (a major causative factor in infant mortality in Africa, for example), health care programmes are often geared to the irradication of the vectors of disease rather than to attempt to cure the disease pattern as and when it presents by chemotherapy. For example, WHO have allocated sums under health care programmes for environmental health such as provision of sanitation and clean water supplies, which ultimately has a clear knock-on effect as far as the consumption of pharmaceuticals is concerned, whilst at the same time the WHO are directing chemotherapeutic programmes against the parasitic diseases engendered by poor environmental conditions. In other words, the policy is to treat the disease as it arises with chemotherapy, whilst at the same time erradicating the causative conditions. Certainly as far as the developing countries are concerned the main pattern of disease probably fits closely to the pharmaceutical consumption pattern itself.

North America — Stress diseases dominate, anxiety neurosis probably being the most prevalent form of illness, and together with cardiac diseases, these stress ailments probably account for as much as one-fifth of the diagnostic work-load of the North American physician. Acute diseases prevailing include the more-common infections, with aches and pains being a frequent ailment.

Western Europe — Cardiac illness dominates, particularly in Germany and France, although the other end of stress ailments, anxiety and depressive illness is not acute or as recurrent here as in North America.

Asia — Asia, like Africa, is dominated by infections and in the latter case communicable disease patterns. Asia is beginning to experience an upsurge in the stress ailments of cardiac and anxiety problems, particularly in Japan and in the more rapidly developing areas of the continents.

3. Health care facilities

A major prerequisite for a well-developed organisation for health care on a national basis as far as outpatient care is concerned is:

1. Provision of adequate diagnostic centres.
2. Provision of pharmaceutical supply-points for drugs.

As far as in-patient care is concerned the main criteria applied are not only the provision of diagnostic and drugs supply but also of accommodation for short- and long-stay patients.

Diagnostic centres
The correlation between medical personnel and *per capita* consumption of products can be readily established and is shown in Table 2.4. However the problems of comparing medical standards using the ratio of population to doctors can be misleading on three counts:

Particularly with respect to the developing countries, the rural populations have little access to medical facilities of any type and for the bulk of the population the provision of health care is a meaningless concept as far as diagnosis and treatment are concerned. Hence the ratios expressed for the developing countries can be reduced if only that proportion of the population to whom medical care is accessible are considered.

The 'usage' of doctors, whether because of their inaccessibility or the expense involved in a consultation, is generally considerably lower in the developing countries. Tolerance of disease is a feature of life and this again reduces usage.

The ratios of specialists to GP's is high in the developed countries where hospital medicine and specialisation make a large proportion of doctors inaccessible to the general public. Hence the ratios shown for the developing countries could be projected upwards to take account of those doctors GPs who are immediately accessible to general patients

Table 2.4. Medical personnel and per capita consumption of products

	Per capita consumption	Ratio of pop. to doctors
Western Europe	37.3	728
North America	35.2	630
Oceania	20.6	785
Eastern Europe	17.0	463
South America	13.1	1753
Asia	6.3	2672
Africa	2.9	7369
Average	14.8	1242

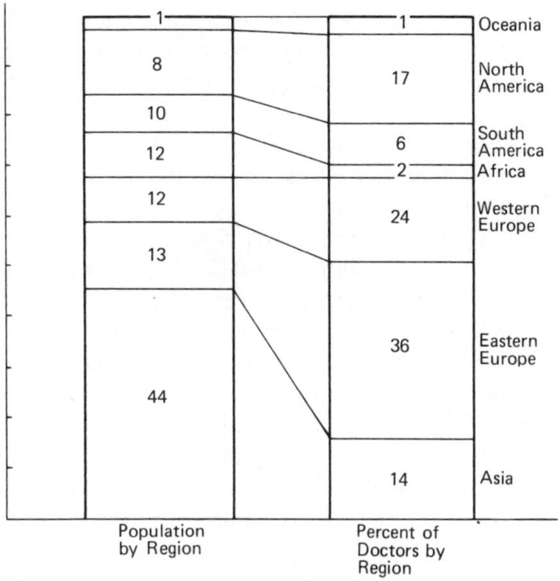

Fig. 2.9. Population and doctor coverage by region (1976).

(Fig. 2.9). Asia and Africa which together have around 56 per cent of the world's population have only 16 per cent of the world's doctors resident within their countries. This situation contrasts strongly with the European situation where only 25 per cent of the world's population are served by 60 per cent of the world's supply of trained medical practitioners. On an individual country level regional statistics on the medical profession assume even greater contrasts. For example in the UK the ratio of population to doctors is around 710:1. Nigeria has a doctor/population ratio of 20,900:1, and Pakistan 4700:1.

Whilst one of the major problems in solving this shortage situation is undoubtedly the provision of adequate training facilities, on the other side of the coin is the problem experienced by countries in the developing world in retaining their trained physicians. Having received a basic training in medicine, many doctors migrate to the more affluent countries for postgraduate training which on paper should ultimately benefit the donor country. The problem arises, however, when the trained specialist wishes to return to his country of origin and finds few openings for his specialisation because his training is geared more to the more-affluent countries' morbidity rates and medical facilities. It is envisaged that this problem will become more serious as qualifications become more internationally recognised and skills more transferable across national boundaries. However not only does this system prevent the less-efficient nations from taking advantage of their own nationals' scarce skills, it also prevents the patient from receiving the chemotherapy associated with that specialist's experienced knowledge.

In most of the countries of the world the pharmacy occupies a position of considerable power with respect to the quality of medical treatment — not only in terms of the physical supply of products on prescription, but also in the diagnosis of illness of a more trivial type on a neighbourhood scale. This latter service offers a method whereby the less-serious cases, in which an OTC product is applicable, can be filtered out of the system and valuable doctor time saved. Often the extent to which neighbourhood medicine operates relates to the accessibility (and costs involved) of the doctors to the patients.

In the developed world sales of OTC products constitute around 10–15 per cent of sales of ethical products and constitute an often lucrative market for the drug producers whose products are prescription-free simple remedies. However, in the developing countries the emphasis is rather less on convenience or advice on trivial illnesses, as on operating a major service in the diagnosis and treatment of a wide range of chronic and acute illnesses. Often the presenting symptoms will warrant a visit to the physician but in many countries this means considerable delay and often considerable expense. The pharmacist is then placed in the position of dispensing scheduled drugs for which he should obtain a prescription. This type of treatment centre poses problems in as much as many of the pharmacies in the developing world are staffed, not by pharmacists, but by inexperienced sales people who are called upon to diagnose and treat conditions that in the more affluent countries might require outpatient treatment at a hospital. This form of treatment also conceals a vast underbelly of infectious conditions and helps to perpetuate many communicable diseases which might otherwise be eradicated. At least this form of treatment involves some informed opinion, whereas much of the illness in the developing countries is self-diagnosed and self-treated in the form of old products or no treatment at all.

However, even where the pharmacy is a powerful weapon (in the right professional hands) against disease, there are all too few of them to make significant inroads into the developing countries' massive health problems. Whereas in Europe the ratio of population to pharmacies ranges from 1600:1 in Holland, at the other end of the scale Egypt with 5000:1 and Indonesia with 123,000:1 reflect the problems of ensuring even a 'neighbourhood' medicine level in the developing countries.

As far as in-patient treatment is concerned an equally grim picture for the developing countries emerges. Whilst in Europe the general level of population to hospital beds is 100–150, in Africa the comparable figure is 850–1000, and in some countries such as Pakistan this figure may be as high as 1850:1. Certainly these figures are reflected in the comparatively low level of in-hospital medicine practised in many of the developing nations. In Europe for example the total drugs bill for the hospital sector will represent 15–20 per cent of the total — reflecting not only a lower consumption rate but also institutional purchasing by tender, which tends significantly to reduce unit dose prices in the developing countries.

Of course these arguments presuppose that a healthy industry exists which can provide enough product of the right kind, at the right price, to provide for most health care expectations. Fortunately this has been possible up to now but there is some evidence that R & D is slowing down in the industry and that in the foreseeable future consumer expectations may not be met by suitable chemotherapy.

4. Health care expectations

Health care expectations are a key determinant of the demand for pharmaceuticals and in the impetus given by the population to government to provide a comprehensive health care system. Overall demand for health care services includes a number of patient-states:

1. Those who sit and suffer either because they are unaware that they are ill or because they are unable to reach a physician.
2. Those who take an OTC preparation having been self-diagnosed or having seen a pharmacist.
3. Those who take the product remaining from their previous bout of illness.
4. Those who visit a doctor for treatment and obtain a prescription.

These various courses of action (or inaction) relate to different people encountering the same health problem. What course of action they take is related largely to (1) their past medical experiences; and (2) their expectations of how they should feel. In general the stoicism demonstrated by the British in the face of illness is gradually giving way to a more relaxed attitude towards going to the doctor and taking the drugs prescribed.

Concomitant with the use of standards of living over the past decade, consumers have broadened their horizons with respect to their quality of life expectations:

1. There is an increased expectancy to feel healthy, fit and happy and a rising intolerance of symptoms which might detract from the above in either physiological or mental-health terms. In other words the threshold point at which illness is recognised is lower and there is a correspondingly strong motivation and will to do something about these symptoms — namely to consult a physician or in cases of readily identifiable 'trivial' problems, to consult a chemist and receive an over-the-counter product. In fact, with respect to the latter form of medicinal, the OTC, growth in this form of product will receive an increasing stimulus, both from the self-prescribers who purchase many of their preparations from the supermarket shelves, and from those who approach the chemist for advice.

It has been reliably estimated that OTC pharmaceuticals accounted for around $900 million sales during 1976 in Western Europe alone, and the figure for 1980 is forecast to be in excess of $1000 million. Assuming a minimum level of expenditure of at least 10 per cent of ethical consumption a world market value of around $4000 million could be computed for this class of product in 1976 — and this is felt to be a low estimate in view of the high level of consumption in those countries where access to medical facilities is difficult.

Generally OTC product usage is restricted to the simpler areas of medicine such as analgesics, cough and cold remedies, laxatives, anti-diahorreals, antacids and skin treatments, and their justification on the market is that they provide those with trivial diseases with simple front-line remedies which in many cases ultimately reduces the call on professional health care personnel. However it is unlikely that the growth in OTC will in any way inhibit the growth of ethical products — rather they will proceed hand-in-hand with OTC products gradually fulfilling the role of the simpler and safer ethical remedies.

Many markets, such as the French and German, have a long history of OTC medicinals, many of which are galenicals, and which are used on a continuous basis in order to maintain health or to deter attacks of trivial disease.

With respect to ethical products in the rising expectancy of health, the role of the prophylactic will undoubtedly assume greater importance — not only to the patient but also to an increasingly overworked medical profession. Where a chronic pattern of disease is noted the repeated visits of a physician, whether it is to check the patient's condition or merely to repeat-prescribe, must place an increasingly intolerable burden on the system in the developed nations. In some respects these visits are 'regulated' in many countries by several factors, as follows: Firstly, the appointments system filters the patient's presenting symptoms and a check is made on whether the condition is of a type which requires treatment; this may screen-out a number of would-be patients.

Secondly, where medical visits cost money, *e.g.*, in the USA, France and Spain, this tends to regulate the flow of patients but produces a socio-economic bias towards the more well-off who can afford repeated visits to the physician. Some systems, notably the French and German, go some way towards solving this problem by reimbursing at least part of the cost of the consultation and moreover a high proportion of the cost of the medicinal prescribed. An additional factor is the time which a doctor's visit requires. This detracts from working time and in many cases places a constraint on the frequency of consultation.

There is undoubtedly evidence to suggest that in the developing countries, at least, the increased expectations of the quality of life is breeding a lack of tolerance for even the more minor symptoms.

2. There is also a rising expectation both on a personal and a corporate basis of an individual's effectiveness linked to job efficiency ensuing from an employee's state of health. In an increasingly competitive environment it is important not only to do the job but to do so in a highly effective, dynamic and aggressive manner. Anything that detracts from this drive for efficiency must be treated and in fact the impetus to many corporate memberships of health schemes has directly stemmed from the desire of the company to ensure the health of employees — not from an altruistic motive but rather as making good economic sense in terms of days lost through illness or inefficient working through illness on the job remaining untreated.

3. Concomitant with the actual efficiency of the employee on the job is the personal appearance which can affect not only the public's reaction to the employee, but also the mood of those who must work in close proximity to the employee. A good, bright, cheerful and healthy appearance is in itself a prerequisite for many professions where the employee must meet the public and increasingly these same standards are being applied to staff whose jobs mean contact within the company.

4. Increasingly emphasis is placed on being a fully participating family member able to shoulder a share of the family's burdens, and

sickness or depression can cause disruption in the family. The normal reaction is now one of forcing the offending member to restore himself to health.

5. Whilst many of these factors stem from the organic movement of society itself towards higher standards of health, it is also true to say that the pharmaceutical industry has contributed significantly to the mood of intolerance towards medical conditions; certainly there is an increased expectation and reliance on the ability of drugs to alleviate and to cure a wider range of conditions than hitherto, particularly with respect to general well-being in the psychological sense. The relief of depressive/anxiety conditions has been one of the chemotherapeutic revolutions of the past decade. Not only have the more-acute conditions been alleviated but also former in-patient conditions have now become out-patient cases, with a consequent reduction in in-patient numbers and an increase in the quality of treatment for such patients.

Moving in parallel with this general upsurge has been the general public's knowledge about medicine and in particular about drugs. Health and medical knowledge are becoming increasingly well developed and the public has higher expectations than ever from the treatment given by the physician.

The focus of the patient is on the drug prescribed rather than on the doctor's advice, support, or other forms of therapy. In this respect education is allowing patients to create a demand for a *brand* of product from the doctor. This is facilitated in chronic cases in particular by the product label bearing the brand name. On subsequent visits the patient tends to ask for the product by name and doctors are now complaining of patient pressure and frequently blame their own over-prescribing, or their prescribing for trivial conditions, on this pressure.

An interesting poll conducted in 1972 by National Opinion Polls established that some 27 per cent of the population is 'very disappointed' if a visit to their doctor fails to ellicit a prescription, and at the other end of the spectrum only 13 per cent stated that they were 'very pleased' not to have received a prescription. This demonstrates the reliance placed by patients on the doctor to prescribe a drug to alleviate the presenting condition and emphasises the heavy dependence of patients on chemotherapy, even when the doctor has not, after careful examination, given the patient a drug.

5. Propensity to purchase

The world is split into two distinct camps where payment of drugs is concerned: (1) **Socialised medicine**, where the patient is given free drugs or must pay a small proportion of the true cost; and (2) **private medicine**, where the patient pays directly for both diagnosis and for drug treatment. Generally, where socialised medicine is concerned, there is an indirect payment system either via federal or state taxes, or an insurance scheme in operation whose deficits are covered by government guarantees. Whichever system is adopted, the rule is established that government is allowed to intervene in the free market forces supplying the drugs. The objective however is not always to provide a higher standard of medical care for the patient, nor to ensure that the state's objectives in facilitating health are carried out in the most efficient manner; but rather that the state obtains the drugs it needs at the cheapest possible price, often irrespective of the quality of those products.

In many respects the state's intervention in fixing prices and reimbursement rates for drugs has a deleterious effect on the system, which in the end reduces the quality of medicine. Not only is the process of fixing prices more complex than many civil servants appear to realise (and this problem is discussed elsewhere), but the implications of trying to pin down producers to minimum price levels is not often realised by governments. The most rational argument advanced by the industry itself is that 'low prices mean low profits mean low R & D ploughback'. The problem here is that few companies actually have an accounting system that can follow a new drug from inception to commercialisation (often a period in excess of eight years) and therefore the apportion of such charges as R & D is a hit-or-miss affair. The fact that the majority of the world's pharmaceutical 'life-savers' are in the hands of probably about 30 companies world-wide means that the industry is by character highly multi-national and hence problems of transfer pricing are complex. The most telling argument is surely that many of the major pharmaceutical companies have 'seen the light' as far as profits are concerned and have diversified out of drugs, often moving into apparently related areas such as cosmetics, only to find that the 'fit' with the new diversification is not as close as was apparent in preacquisition manoeuvres, and that the margins and methods of doing business are both somewhat less than satisfactory, compared with pharmaceuticals in their heyday of the late '50s early '60s. The main drive of the government has been directed in two directions, prices and generics.

Prices (and hence profits) — The main area apart from controlling both the entry and the established market prices of products has been attempts to stimulate competition amongst companies sometimes by allowing — as has happened in the UK — the government to grant compulsory licenses to copiers who will normally undertake to price their products below the originator's prices. However, whilst the government on one hand is trying to stimulate competition it is quite often restricting the means by which companies communicate their competitive offerings to the prescriber. In the UK in particular, efforts are being made to limit the amount of promotion to a fixed percentage of the turnover. One of the effects of this may well be to limit the amount of information the prescriber has at his disposal to make a cost-effective decision.

Generics — This is a highly contentious area which has bubbled quietly away for at least a decade. The objective of government is to force prescribers to specify products by the general chemical name of the product, rather than the brand, thus allowing the pharmacist to fill the script from the cheapest available product. This does not benefit either the consumer or the doctor — or in many cases the pharmacist, who may even prefer to dispense the branded product because of the higher mark-up involved. Nor does it ultimately benefit the government because more frequently than not the generic product has been imported from countries such as Italy, Poland or Hungary and paid for in foreign currency, whereas the product against whom it is competing is probably domestically produced.

In fact many of the major US corporations have quietly constructed generic product lines which they market together with their ordinary line of branded products. Particularly with respect to institutional purchasing, generic drugs often make sense, providing the origins of the product are known and respected, and the price differential is such that discounts lost through 'small parcel' purchases of branded products from a wide range of producers, do not balance up the savings.

Many countries, such as the UK and the USA have published GMP (Good Manufacturing) codes which enforce a minimum standard on producers who hope to market in these countries. These regulations apply both to domestic and to foreign producers; for example, the Federal Drugs Administration have inspectors located in Europe and elsewhere to check prospective exporter's premises and manufacturing practices. Whilst the consequence of importation, is in many cases cheaper substitutes, it also means that the costs of patrolling product standards becomes significantly higher; and hence this form of cost saving would become self-defeating if the real cost of its implementation could be demonstrated.

Overall socialised medicine can only be justifiedof its coverage is 100 per cent of the population and its contributions are not so burdensome as to be cost-ineffective compared to private systems — however these contributions are calculated. On the whole, private medical systems are at their best when tandomised with a socialised system.

Although access to GPs and outpatient treatment can be within the reach of the population as a whole (provided that some provision is made for chronic cases) in general in-patient treatment is prohibitively expensive, particularly in chronic or surgical cases where long-stay complex treatment is required. Unfortunately for the drug industry, the image of high-cost private treatment invariably is linked with a pharmaceutical industry 'battening on the misfortunes of the sick'. Quite frequently nothing would be further from the truth with the cost of drugs being a small proportion of the patient's cost of stay — often the cost of chemotherapy being exceeded by that of laundry or meals — and authorities would do well to review these cost components in the patient's daily rate.

However, institutional purchases in the developed countries may only constitute 15–20 per cent, at most, of the total country's drug bill. In the developing nations government purchases may constitute around 70 per cent of the total consumption. Fortunately most of these countries have adopted a socialised approach to medicinals, however restricted their outlets for these drugs may be. As an alternative to dealing with the multi-nationals, many of the developing countries have placed tenders for their basic drug requirements which have been won by the Eastern European countries, primarily in the anti-infective/anti-bacterial areas. This has the effect certainly of reducing the overall drug bill for the more frequently used items such as antibiotics, but many of the multi-nationals who would otherwise be interested in marketing to these countries have shied away from doing business because of the restricted categories of product they may be allowed to market.

Undoubtedly these developing countries may purchase much of their total requirements from one source, say the COMECON countries. However, it would be very short-sighted indeed to totally exclude the multi-nationals for two major reasons. Firstly, the R & D potential of the multi-national companies considerably outweighs that (if any) of the COMECON producers, who are primarily interested in taking up patent-expired products, developing in many cases highly efficient large-scale production, and exporting bulk and finished products to the developing world. Certainly, so long as the multi-national companies are prepared to supply the less-frequently used products, then this policy may save the developing countries some money. The problem arises, however, when a developing group of developing nations requires drugs specific to their own unique morbidity patterns. Where are these drugs to come from? Certainly not from the COMECON producers, or from indigenous production. Rather they must (as they have been in the past) be developed from the resources held by the multinational companies who may prove unwilling to risk shareholders' cash on a venture in a country which may be commercially unexploitable in other ways.

Secondly, the objectives of countries, developed or developing, is to create a viable production base for a domestic pharmaceutical industry, usually starting with 'finishing'. Most countries progress to formulation and eventually to the production of raw materials. Usually this final stage is gained from joint ventures with multi-national companies who see that their future in the developing world must be in partnership with the indigenous industry. More often than not this type of translation of ownership is carried out on an orderly and progressive basis with the indigenous population benefiting greatly from the know-how in both production and marketing of their multi-national partner. However, where the source of supply is the COMECON countries this know-how and co-operation may not be forthcoming or may cover only a small percentage of the country's overall pharmaceutical needs.

There have been many suggestions in the past that groups of developing countries should get together to set up a type of informal common market in pharmaceuticals to produce a restricted range of the most frequently used products on a co-operative basis, co-ordinating production on patent expired drugs which would be marketed throughout the group's markets under their generic names. As recently as April/May 1976 this programme was put forward at a UNIDO conference attended by 22 developing countries representing aggregate pharmaceutical sales of $3.9 billion.

A similar scheme has been put forward by OECD for the less-rich countries of Europe, such as Turkey, Greece, Portugal and Spain.

The problem with this type of organisation is not only the administration of the system but the decisions on what goes into the list of products to be jointly produced and — even more significantly — where these products are to be produced.

Some countries, such as India, have recognised the vital role played by foreign-owned pharmaceutical companies and the comparative lack of resources and technical know-how in the Indian public sector ensure foreign-owned company licenses for the production of bulk drugs urgently required locally such as anti-malarials. In 1974 the Hathi

Committee, set up to study the health care service, recommended the abolition of brand names and the substitution of generic names. However, this policy has now been watered-down by negotiation and in fact producers who are marketing the list of 117 compounds recognised as essential by the committee will gain certain concessions in return for price reductions. This is an orderly and reasoned method of reducing the drug bill. In complete contrast, Pakistan has adopted a very tough stand on brand names, prohibiting them altogether and pledging to encourage domestic drug production at the expense of foreign companies. The direct result has been the pulling out of Pakistan of many of the foreign-owned companies, resulting in a reduction in the products available.

Many countries have taken a less drastic stand but still produce significant savings in their drug bill. Turkey, for example, has adopted the approach of controlling the costs of imported bulk material and stipulating the profit margins of both wholesalers and pharmacists. In Portugal the prices of domestic producers operate on a separate structure from that of the foreign importers. Generally, indigenously produced products are priced on the basis of cost plus 30 per cent. For imports the price is based on the price charged in the country of origin reduced by 35 per cent to establish a baseline for wholesaler and pharmacy mark-ups. In Spain the pharmacist is obliged to dispense drugs in the producer's own packs and producer's profits are limited by law to 15 per cent and the wholesaler's to 12 per cent on the retailer's buying price. At the other extreme Sweden's pharmacists have been nationalised and prices are strictly controlled, as is doctor's prescribing.

Whatever system of price determination and control is applied, it should be backed-up by strong controls on the doctor's prescribing and possibly on the mark-ups of the wholesalers and the retailers.

3 Legislation and the Industry

Estimates made prior to the introduction of the NHS in the UK indicated that the cost of funding the service would be of the order of £140–190 million per year, and at that level would not represent a heavy financial burden on the taxpayer. Currently the cost of the NHS is in excess of £5000 million or around 5.4 per cent of GNP, and recent data have indicated that NHS expenditure has risen more than 35 per cent faster than GNP since 1960.

The cost of drugs alone to the NHS is in the region of £500 million, although even in a period of high inflation the percentage of the overall NHS costs accounted for by drug expenditure has dropped from 11.2 per cent in 1966 to its current figure of around 9 per cent. Undoubtedly the system has been subject to severe inflationary influences since its inception, but the real blame for the situation must lie squarely at the feet of the planners of the original service, who based their cost estimates on three principles:

1. That the normal state of the individual is one of health and by implication illness of any type, acute or chronic, is abnormal in the population.
2. If a comprehensive health care system became available to all, irrespective of income level, there would be a gradual improvement in the level of the nation's health, resulting in a progressive decline in the overall demand for health care over time.
3. Hence the costs of funding the service would probably level off in the short/medium term, and might even decline in the longer term.

Successive governments have wrestled with the problems built into the NHS at the design stage by adherence to such fundamental misconceptions. Their response to the challenge has been piecemeal, with brush-fire management, apparently without a concerted plan for dealing with the seemingly irrevocable slide of the NHS towards chaos and perhaps even eventual dissolution.

Instead of rethinking the base philosophy behind the service's purpose and objectives, the main thrust of the bureaucrats has been to attack the drugs bill, which since the NHS's inception has rarely exceeded 12 per cent of the total NHS expenditure; and which, if the volume of product consumed is compared on an international basis, demonstrates without doubt that the NHS has secured the most favourable price structures for the majority of drugs in common use. The UK government has been in the forefront of the 'bash the drug industry brigade', maintaining that the industry is 'battening on the misfortunes of the sick' and 'generating huge profits out of suffering and illness' — charges which for various reasons the industry has found as difficult to refute as the government would to prove.

The whole problem of drug control is obscured by a smokescreen of emotional charge and countercharge and needs to be examined objectively. Theoretically, the government's problem in reducing the drugs bill (if this is the administrations real objective) will ultimately be solved under the two pronged attack on the industry which is currently underway. The methods used are:

1. Indirect controls over the doctor/patient relationship in terms of: (*a*) Limiting the freedom of the doctor to prescribe; and (*b*) curbing the strength of patient demand for treatment.
2. Direct controls over the industry by: (*a*) Control over drug pricing; and (*b*) limiting the numbers of new products entering the market, whilst subjecting existing products to ongoing evaluation.

As far as the more direct means are concerned the model of the NHS shown in Fig. 3.1, although based on the UK system, broadly highlights the European and North American market environments.

LIMITS TO PRESCRIBER'S FREEDOM TO TREAT

Since the socialised medical systems of the developed world cannot function without doctors, all governments, almost without exception, have had to take a soft line with the profession, and this has certainly been reflected in their approach to direct controls on this group. Few authorities, whether government or Social Security Insurance Funds, have dared hitherto to press the case either for a reduction in prescribing or for access to physicians to be reduced, too strongly, and those that have taken the bit between their teeth have invariably met with failure.

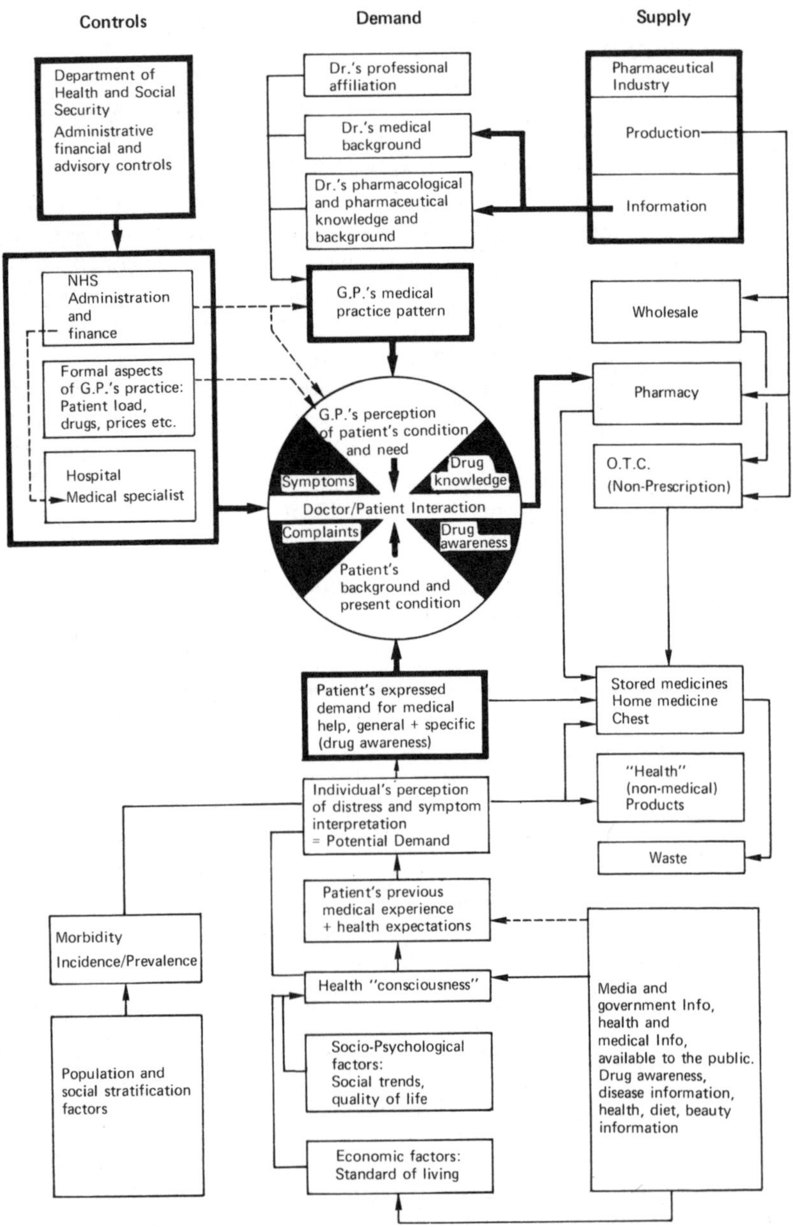

Fig. 3.1. Process of demand formation (micro-level). United Kingdom.

Overprescribing is a problem ostensibly dealt with most effectively by the doctors themselves operating in a self-regulatory regularity capacity. In the UK this system is based on a local average cost per script being calculated for monitored diagnosis. Doctors exceeding the average are cautioned, and persistent offenders are then subject to a medical 'court' which has powers to fine. However, in the UK the number of doctors actually fined each year rarely achieves double figures.

In Europe where health care is primarily in the hands of Private Insurance Funds, attempts are made to regulate the cost per script using a similar method to the UK and with about the same success. In Germany, for example, there is a proposal under the Health Care Insurance Expenditure Act which would impose maximum expenditure outlays on individual physicians for fixed periods, linked to a closely vetted list of approved drugs largely based on price. At the end of each period any overages on prescription costs would be deducted from the other component of the cost outlay — the doctor's salary. Needless to say the German doctor is not overjoyed at this prospect, and with the political muscle that can be mobilised by this group there is little possibility of this plan being implemented.

However, European governments in many cases must share the blame for many of the overprescribing 'excesses' of doctors, and one of the main problems involved in cutting-down the size of scripts lies in the legislative stipulations as to pack sizes. In most European countries ethical products must be dispensed by law in the manufacturer's original and unopened pack (Table 3.1). This has been due to regulations governing patient reimbursement, but it also prevents the pharmacist from buying in bulk and filling the script from a large dispensing pack. Hence there are no economies of scale: a pharmacist faced with a script for 30 tablets cannot supply from a dispensing pack of 1000, which he has secured from the manufacturer at a considerable discount, thereby benefitting both the patient and the Health Fund by passing on the savings involved in bulk buying.

In addition, more often than not, the script would be dispensed using a pack approximating in size to the number of tablets specified — a process which usually involves an excess of products given over the prescribed level, the overage representing a considerable loss both to patient and to Health Care Fund.

In many cases the doctor, not aware of the original pack sizes endorses the script 'original pack size' relying on the pharmacist to dispense the nearest size available. Not only does this policy militate

Table 3.1. European pack dispensing policies

	Pack breaking	
	Permitted	Prohibited
Austria		X
Belgium		X
Denmark		X
Finland		X
France		X
West Germany		X
Ireland	X	
Italy		X
Holland	X	
Norway		X
Portugal		X
Spain		X
Sweden		X
Switzerland		X
UK	X	

against cost savings, and facilitate overprescribing, such practices mean that even long established international brands are marketed throughout Europe in different pack sizes for each country, incurring additional production costs for the multi-nationals — costs which invariably are passed onto the 'consumer' by way of higher prices. Whilst the effects on drug usage are unclear there seems to be little doubt that this method of prescribing is not cost-effective.

Some doubts have also been expressed that the 'freedom' of prescribing encouraged by dispensing packs may lead to overprescribing by physicians by allowing too much flexibility. For example, during 1976 in the UK over 2,000 kgs. of surplus drugs were returned to pharmacists under a scheme designed to rid households of dangerous and unwanted drugs. Much of this was undoubtedly due to overprescribing, though to be fair a proportion could have resulted from patient failure to complete their full course of treatment. Some spectacular cases of overprescribing have been brought to light by the Irish Working Party on Prescribing and Dispensing, which in 1976 identified one script calling for 20 bottles of cough mixture, and another which specified 30 bottles of nasal drops. Whilst most overprescribing takes a less extreme form it is a recurrent problem, which if treated seriously by the authorities could produce significant savings on the drugs bill without any lowering in the standard of health care.

In the USA the position concerning overprescribing is somewhat different. Until the advent of Federally funded medical schemes (Medicare/Medicaid) overprescribing was controlled by the patient himself by his own ability to pay for medicinals. However, the growth in Medicaid/Medicare (currently costing the US Government $1500 million per year), where the patient receives free treatment and drugs has led to a situation where the government has described prescribing abuses as 'scandalous'. A recent (1976) Senate committee reported not only widespread abuses in the form of overprescribing, but also an upsurge under the socialised system of unnecessary prescriptions. The US response has been to set up a watchdog body to scrutinise Medicare/Medicaid expenses at a cost which is reported to be in excess of $25 million.

REDUCING PATIENT DEMAND

The alternative to reducing the drugs bill — curbing patient demand — has always been attractive to governments, particularly those who either directly fund socialised medical health care or who have guaranteed to fund the deficits of the Private Health Insurance funds. The most obvious way of limiting patient demand is to charge a fee for consultations and impose payments on patients for drugs prescribed. Both have achieved limited success, as most health care funds have systems of reimbursement to patients based on a percentage of the total which takes much of the financial sting out of the system. However, the patient may receive reimbursement only after the full fees have been paid under most systems, and it is felt that the system offers a minor, but effective, brake on the more trivial consultations and drug therapies.

Interestingly enough, probably the most effective controls over drug costs are operated informally by the doctors themselves without prompting by the authorities. This is done by the doctors placing barriers between themselves and their would-be patients, often abetted by governments prepared to give cash concessions and allowances for the provision of auxiliary staff who are used by the doctors to filter out the more trivial cases which need not be seen by the doctor, and who actively discourage patients from requesting home visits. Faced with a barrage of questions regarding his condition the patient may be discouraged from coming to the surgery and in this way the auxiliary regulates the flow of patients into the surgery by applying a prediagnostic check on the presenting symptoms of the patient's illness.

Whilst the overall effects of this system has probably been to reduce significantly the doctor's workload, it has interposed a layman between the doctor and the patient and inevitably must lead to an overall deterioration in the quality of the doctor/patient interaction, as well as imposing extra financial constraints in the system by the employment of increasing numbers of auxiliary staff to cope with an appointments system. Despite this dampening effect on demand, consumption continues to rise, although probably more slowly than it would if access to the physician had remained free and unconditional.

That an increase is still taking place at all is mainly due to the failure of the government to anticipate and prevent the groundswell of demand for health care in the general populace, a demand which has been characterised by a remarkable shift in the attitude of the population towards illness in general, discussed more fully in Chapter 2. In many cases the only really effective demand restraints lie in the more direct controls imposed by government and health care funds on the industry itself.

EFFECTS OF STRINGENT REGISTRATION OF NEW DRUGS

In terms of registration procedures, governments have progressively applied more rigorous controls over the introduction of new products into the markets. Often these controls have been extended through time to cover stringent evaluations of established products, sometimes with the result that they are withdrawn from the market.

The pre- and post-launch evaluations have become an increasing cost burden on the companies, a burden which most companies have succeeded in passing onto the health care funding agency by means of raising prices. The growth in regulation governing the quality, safety and efficacy of drugs has caused the industry considerable problems. One major consequence has been the lengthening of the time taken between discovery and commercialisation. It has been reliably estimated that a major drug will take between 7–8 years from screening to launch, and during this time will cost the company an estimated $50 million. Whilst this increases the costs of development it has also a more serious side-effect — that of denying to patients in some cases potential life-saving drugs.

In comparing the UK, which is still considered by many to be relatively liberal in respect of new drug legislation, with the USA, where there are considerably harsher market entry regulations, it can be demonstrated that many life-saving products (some of which originate from US multi-nationals) are launched in the UK well in advance of their entry into the USA.

A comparison of the introduction of 82 drugs into the UK and US markets was made for the period 1962–71, by the US Pharmaceutical Manufacturing Association:

	UK	*US*	*Simul-taneous*	*TOTALS*
AGGREGATE (BOTH COUNTRIES)	43	25	14	82
ONLY 1 COUNTRY	77	21	–	98

Source: PMA Fact Book

Quite clearly, the UK, despite being a market six times smaller than the US, has allowed almost twice the number of launches made in the US market, with 14 products being launched simultaneously into the UK/US markets. In fact, of the 98 products launched in the two countries during the period 1962–71, the UK market absorbed almost four times the US launch total.

The Food and Drug Administration (FDA) in the USA, which controls the admission of new products into the market, has been accused by doctors and the industry alike of not only operating stringent regulations, but also of operating them inefficiently, to the ultimate disadvantage of the consumer, as the launches of significant new products in the USA have been reduced to a trickle. Owing to the FDA's stringent regulations an average of only 15 new single entities per year were launched on to the US market between 1970 and 1975.

The effect of such harsh entry requirements on the industry in the USA has been not only to increase considerably the expense of progressing commercially interesting products through the R and D process, but also to eliminate very early in the R & D programme products which, although not potentially large profit-earners, would have a significant therapeutic effect in the treatment of less-prevalent conditions where usage is low but nevertheless chemotherapy is essential. There is growing evidence that US companies are cutting back on basic research into new single entities to concentrate more resources on defensive R & D wherein improvements are made to existing products in order to protect their position in the market, both in terms of commercial threats and regulatory body evaluations.

Ultimately this regression will significantly affect the numbers and quality of new innovatory drugs entering the market.

In a recent survey by the PMA in the USA, it was computed that US companies controlled a world-wide R & D expenditure in the region of over $1150 million, yet only one US company appeared in the top five companies launching new products during 1976:

	No. of new products
Roche (Swiss)	60
Hoechst (West Germany)	53
Bristol Myers (US)	45
Boehringer Ingleheim (West Germany)	44
Ciba-Geigy (Swiss)	40

According to the same PMA survey the R & D expenditure in 1976 for US companies rose only 8.4 percent over the previous year. Since inflation in R & D was computed by the PMA to be in the region of 15 percent then the real change in 1976 over 1975 was of the order of a 6–7 percent decrease. Hence it could be postulated that the actual productivity in R & D in US companies must be falling.

As far as registration in Europe is concerned, it was only in 1976 that 'harmonisation' of the EEC regulations (originally laid down in 1965) was adopted for the member countries. Even so, the intention is for those regulations to take effect not before 1980. Broadly these will: (1) harmonise registration procedures and requirements between countries; and (2) eliminate import/export controls over pharmaceuticals in the EEC.

In many cases the ten-year transition period between laying down and adoption has meant that many of the member states such as West Germany and UK have taken the opportunity of revising their registration procedures to fit the EEC regulations. Thus the transition for these countries will be smoother. The question arises, however, of whether these regulations could act to limit the number of useful products coming into the market. Certainly many of the adopting countries have not only accepted the EEC regulations but have actually gone beyond them in terms of stringency. This has of course had the general effect of upgrading the general level of standards of testing in the EEC countries, but has done very little towards a complete standardisation of EEC regulations as originally envisaged.

It is intended that considerable control powers are vested in the Committee on Proprietory Medical Products of the EEC which is charged with control over the granting, suspension and withdrawal of registration. In effect the EEC intends legislation to cover not only new products, but also retrospective launches, *i.e.*, reviewing products already on the market. This will impose a considerable burden of defensive R & D on the industry in Europe and may well result in a significant reduction of innovation along the lines of the US decline over the next decade. It seems as if the European situation may well parallel that in operation in Japan today, where there is a well-established system of drug efficacy reviews on established products. During 1976 alone over 1,300 products were assessed and as a result around 60 were recommended for withdrawal. Since the programme started in Japan a total of just under 6,500 products have been reviewed, resulting in a withdrawal of just under 400.

As these various legislative procedures focusing on the evaluation of new and established products get underway, there can be little doubt that it will have a negative effect on the research policies and budgets of companies. Less time will be spent on basic research into disease and more resources will be put into searching for improvements to existing products — i.e., defensive development rather than research *per se*. This will not only have the effect of reducing the numbers of new products coming onto the market but may well also significantly lower the innovative capacity of the industry through time.

PRICE AS A DEMAND CURB

Price is still a key plank in most governments cost-control mechanisms for the health care industry, and in fact the issue of pricing has had to become a major preoccupation of the industry over the past decade.

In the USA, since the inception of Medicare/Medicaid, the government has really woken up to the problems of pricing and margins at all levels in production and distribution, and is attacking prices on two broad fronts. Firstly, there is a real move to control price-levels as a pre- *and* post-launch control. Currently five major US corporations, Eli Lilly, MSD, Abbott, Bristol Myers and Smith-Kline are contesting the Government Accounting Office's right of access to confidential drug cost and drug pricing data on their products. The government feels justified in asking for such information from the companies as it reimburses Medicare/Medicaid drug programmes to the tune of $1500 million per year, and is concerned that it is being overcharged for supplies. In fact the US government is maintaining that it has a contractual right of access to such information.

The companies are rightly wary of such moves, not only because it is felt that this request is merely the thin end of the wedge as far as disclosure is concerned, but also because they are not impressed by the government's ability to keep such information confidential, and would certainly be fearful lest the information were leaked to Congressional and Senate committees and thereby would become public property. Apart from these very real fears, the industry has stated very clearly that such information which exists on the costs of individual products are rough estimates only, and that because of problems of apportionment of costs 'in house' the real costs of products cannot be accurately established. As far as the relationship of costs to prices are concerned MSD's Vice President of Finance recently went on record as stating that his own company's prices were determined less by actual costs of production than by comparison with competing products. In other words, prices are often fixed irrespective of costs and government access to data would not place them in a true position to assess the industries pricing policies.

Equally agressive on pricing has been the EEC, which apart from taking a number of companies to court, e.g., Roche, over their pricing policies, are intending to publicise the final prices at which major bulk business is won by companies for member states. It is apparently doing so in the hope that eventually a European Standard Price will be set up for most major EEC drugs. Under the terms of an EEC directive due for enforcement in mid-1978 supply contracts awarded by National Health Care Schemes of member countries must be drafted in conformity with EEC directives, and where the tender price exceeds 200,000 units of account ($220,000) it must be published in the official journal together with the technical specifications. This will have the effect of both publicising tender prices and standardising levels of efficacy throughout the EEC.

Just as significantly for price in the EEC is the authority's encouragement of increased price competition in the market via what are termed 'parallel imports' and also via the encouragement of generics.

Parallel-importing originated in Holland when with official government blessing a Dutch wholesaler CENTRAFARM imported Roche psychotropics, purchased legally from UK wholesalers, and resold them to pharmacists in Holland at below the Roche operating subsidiary price in that country. In fact Valium from the UK is priced at

$1.60 whereas that supplied by Roche (Holland) is priced at $1.98. The Dutch government has gone one step further by introducing a published list of prices of parallel imports of pharmaceuticals, thereby introducing a two-tier reimbursement system.

The EEC's reaction to this has been to condone the Dutch government's activities, whilst at the same time accusing another EEC member, Italy, of maintaining drug prices at an artificially low level, using as its reason, that low drug prices inhibit new product launches. In addition the EEC is exhorting the Italians to export their drugs at low prices to other EEC countries in order to try to bring down prices of drugs within the EEC. So on the one hand the EEC laws are used to encourage parallel-importing, which reduces prices in Holland (under an EEC directive against restraint of trade), and at the same time forcing Italian producers to raise prices to encourage innovation. There seem to be a number of inconsistencies in these policies.

As a second point on prices both American and European governments have persisted in their encouragement of low price generics, in the hope that the provision of low-cost competition to the established leaders will encourage price-cutting. There is some evidence that, for example, in the USA, whilst the volume of generic scripts is increasing, the prices of established brands are remaining steady, and because of the increases in the size of scripts, branded business is expanding. Over the past five years the volume of generic prescriptions in the USA has increased by 25 percent, whereas branded products have increased by only 8 per cent.

In the USA the main generics argument has revolved around the contention that the pharmacist should have the right to substitute a lower-priced generic equivalent of a branded drug. In 1977 pharmacists in many states have the right of substitution unless specifically instructed by the prescriber. The government has now drawn up a listing of over 1,600 generic equivalent products which are marketed by reliable producers, and which can be used as substitutes for branded products.

In the medium to long term, government activity in the area of generics is likely to arouse even more controversy. A report issued by the Federal Trade Commission in 1977 has recommended that pharmaceutical trademarks should not be renewable after 20 years in order to encourage free market competition, and in addition is providing strong federal support for state activities designed to repeal the anti-substitution laws. In the near future a specially commissioned paper on substitution and formulatory listings of interchangeable products is expected from the FDA, and could provide a more accurate guide than is emerging under the so-called Maximum Allowable Cost programme instigated by the Federal Government.

In the EEC there is evidence that although governments and Health Insurance Funds are keen to instigate cost-saving generics plans, the prescribers and the pharmacists are less than enthusiastic. With respect to the prescriber, there is no financial incentive for the doctor to prescribe generics and he is probably lothe to depart from his well-tried armoury of brand names associated with reputable companies. Although the image of generics has improved since the regulations governing registration were tightened up, until recently doctors have viewed themselves as being at least partly liable if a product they prescribed should be faulty.

In the EEC countries, at least, this fear has been removed by the recent adoption of new product liability regulations, which make producers directly liable to consumers for product failures. Under these new proposals, a defendent producer must prove that the product was not defective when it left his control. The situation is reversed in the USA, where the influenced plaintiff must prove that the product was defective when it left the manufacturer. Furthermore, under EEC legislation the producer is liable even for those defects that could not be foreseen 'in the light of the scientific and technical developments' at the time the product was launched. Whilst this legislation may well produce in prescribers a feeling of security and hence a more relaxed attitude towards the prescription and dispensing of generics; it may also deter some of those generics producers who were operating close to tolerable limits of safety and efficacy from putting their products onto the market.

The more radical administrations in Europe have proposed that they, or the Health Insurance Funds, purchase drugs directly from producers for dispensing directly to patients. However, the more middle-of-the-road approach has been to stipulate generic labelling on the products (together with the brand name) and to draw prescribers' attention to the cost comparisons between the branded and the generic equivalents in terms of treatment costs.

The response by the industry to this onslaught on prices has been twofold. Firstly, to maintain, and wherever justified, to increase drug prices on their branded products. The producers have refused to be panicked by external pressures. In fact they have begun to fight back aggressively by moving themselves into the generics area *via* 'house generics'.

American Cyanamid, Eli Lilly and Smith Kline, all major reputable US drug companies, have moved into the 'house generics' business, and their level of success is understood to be significant. For example, American Cyanamid launched a range of 80 generic products onto the US market in 1975, and intend to increase this range to 120 by the end of 1977, indicating their positive expectations in this area.

In many respects the movement of these highly ethical and reputable drug houses into the generics business is both a commercial necessity, as far as preserving their own profitability is concerned, as well as being highly desirable from the wider public interest angle. Certainly these companies, and others who may follow, have brought certain standards of safety and efficacy into play in the generics market which were missing when this market was solely the province of the small distributor who imported his product lines from Eastern Europe or Italy. By offering the prescriber a choice between branded or generic products the companies are really asking the doctor to make a choice based purely on economics, rather than previously where the trade-off for a lower price was reduced efficacy and safety.

As far as the developing world is concerned the generics problem is a thorny one. On the one hand, in order to avoid a drugs famine in certain therapeutic areas these countries cannot afford to alienate the multi-national companies from their markets. Undoubtedly the radical proposals for the importation of cheap bulk drugs from Eastern Europe to cover major therapeutic areas, whilst developing indigenous pharmaceutical production and formulation facilities, may be viable for some 'hard line' countries, but it would certainly drive away the multinationals from these countries, and the end-result would be significant gaps in their essential drugs supplies.

The WHO has entered this contentious area with a recent report in 1976 which outlined a list of around 150 basic substances which, it is hoped, will be sufficient to cover the two basic levels of health care named by the developing world: (1) Products for the relief of disease while the diagnostic facilities are non-existent or primitive; and (2) Products, slightly more sophisticated, for treatment where diagnostic facilities are existent.

The *rationale* for the development of such listing is that where limited resources, not only of funds, but also of storage, distribution and medical manpower, are available, then it is much easier to handle a small number of products in large quantities, than a large variety of products in smaller quantities. As far as production is concerned, those countries that possess the know-how and the resources to develop their own industry could concentrate on producing a limited number of drugs which have recognisable therapeutic advantages to the country concerned. The Committee emphasised that the listing was based on health criteria only, and the objectives were to supply state health services with economical basic products — and not to limit the activities of the drug companies. However, it must be conceded that the adoption of such a list must influence that country's prescribers towards the indigenously produced low-cost products.

Initially such a programme may well produce a welcome expansion of business for the multi-national companies in those countries adopting the list, in as much as those that cooperate and give production and marketing priorities to the recommended drugs, may well facilitate the expansion of health care into areas where none hitherto existed, thus creating and taking advantage of an opportunity to expand their business. However, ultimately the state will wish to be involved in the production of the drugs with intervention levels ranging from simply a shareholding in the business to eventual outright nationalisation of the multi-national's assets.

Certainly the other UN bodies involved in health care, UNIDO and UNCTAD, have not taken the WHO line of co-existence with the multi-nationals. In 1976 UNIDO sponsored a conference, attended by 22 developing countries on the key topic 'Drug Technology without Profits' — which suggested that drug technology transfer should be encouraged to circumvent commercial companies' operations in Third World countries. It also adopted a listing of basic products, but more significantly recommended the abolution of brand names and the promotion of generic prescribing in Third World countries. UNCTAD has also proposed greater co-operation between developing countries in a 1975 report which severely criticised the multi-nationals' role in the drug industry.

Balanced against this the basic listing of the WHO may be viewed by the more suspicious companies, not as an opportunity, but as a direct threat to their established activities in the countries of the developing world. However, high-volume local production of basic drugs should not greatly affect the majority of the multi-nationals, but would be a severe blow to those COMECON countries whose exports of bulk antibiotics have traditionally provided them with a revenue base from which to snipe at the market success of the more-established multi-nationals in the more-lucrative specialist areas.

What would really worry the multi-national companies is the prospect of government intervention on two fronts; the abolition of brand names, together with a restriction in the repatriation of profits. For example, in 1973 Pakistan enacted the 'Generic Names Act' which banned brand names. The end result was the flooding of the market by a number of spurious drugs, many of which had problems of efficacy and safety. This eventually led to prescribers reverting back to branded products produced by reputable manufacturers, in fact strengthening the multi-nationals' market penetration in many cases.

The concentration of legislation in the developed world has undoubtedly been directed at two areas: (1) Raising standards of drug safety and efficacy; and (2) reducing prices, and thereby relieving hard-pressed health care bodies. However, the two are closely interlinked. Almost inevitably as soon as standards are made more stringent, then costs rise. Rising costs are a powerful argument for justifying price increases. Thus, in this particular area, governments have to adhere to a balance between acceptable standards of drug production and prices that reflect the higher social responsibilities thrust upon the industry by governments.

4 Politics and Prices – Background

CONCERN IN THE NHS

Pharmaceutical prices are regarded with concern in most countries.[1] One of the first nations to examine formally the size of its drug bill was the UK. The probable reason why the British drug industry was subject to government scrutiny relatively earlier than its counterparts elsewhere was its relationship with the National Health Service (NHS). In the UK the vast majority of prescriptions are written under the NHS and are mainly paid for by the government (Fig 4.1). As virtual sole purchaser (or monopsonist) of the industry's output it was a natural consequence that the government should be interested in the prices of the products for which it was paying. This was reinforced by the fact that the cost of the NHS rose after its inception and continued to rise. This was contrary to the belief of some of its founders who alleged that the creation of the NHS would result in fewer resources being spent on health care.[2]

In addition, in the initial years expenditure on pharmaceuticals rose as a percentage of the total NHS costs. In 1952 total NHS expenditure at £523 million was 9.6 per cent higher than its 1950 level of £477 million. Expenditure on pharmaceutical services, however, had risen from £40 million to £55 million in the same period. An increase of 37.5 per cent, nearly four times as great a rise as that for the NHS as a whole.

Brian Abel-Smith and Richard Titmuss conducted an investigation into the factors accounting for the rise of pharmaceutical service expenditure between 1949 and 1953/54. This was carried out on behalf of the Guillebaud Committee, which reported in 1956.[3] They concluded that about one-third of the rise was due to increased drug consumption since the inception of the NHS, and a similar proportion to the introduction of new and expensive drugs, particularly antibiotics — a trend reflected by the increased prescribing of branded drugs. The remaining causes were not specified. A further government committee

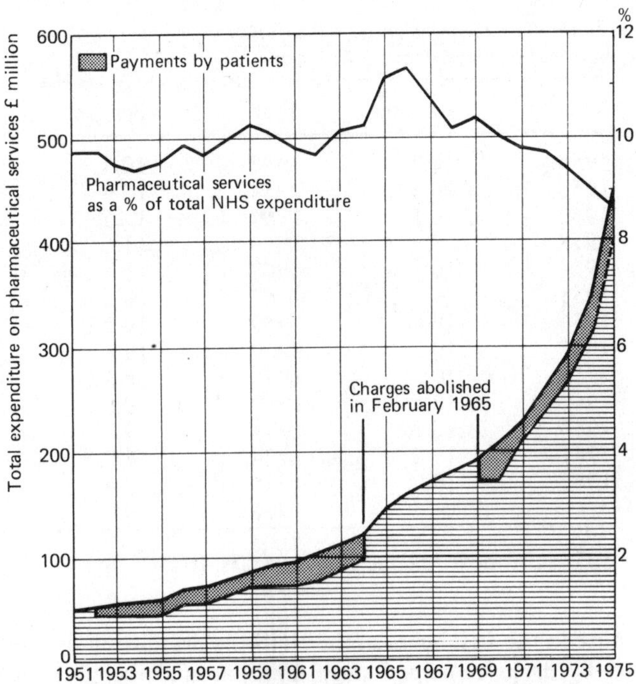

Fig. 4.1. Total expenditure on pharmaceutical services and amounts raised by prescription charges. United Kingdom.

Source: Compendium of Health Statistics, Office of Health Economics (2nd edition, 1977).

was then set up, the Hinchcliffe Committee,[4] whose terms of reference specifically directed it to have 'regard to the increase in the cost of prescriptions issued under the NHS, to investigate the factors contributing to this cost and to make recommendations'. Hinchcliffe examined the proportion of total NHS expenditure incurred by the pharmaceutical services and concluded that the 'figures do not support the general belief that the cost of the pharmaceutical service is increasing at a much faster rate than that of other branches of the NHS or that it is absorbing an increasing share in the total cost of the Service'.[5]

This conclusion is substantiated in Table 4.1 and in Fig. 4.1. These show that apart from the disproportionate rise in pharmaceutical

Table 4.1. Proportion of NHS expenditure on pharmaceutical services. United Kingdom

Year	Per cent	Year	Per cent
1950	8.4	1963	10.5
1951	10.4	1964	10.6
1952	10.5	1965	11.5
1953	9.9	1966	11.6
1954	10.1	1967	11.1
1955	9.9	1968	10.6
1956	10.6	1969	10.9
1957	10.3	1970	10.6
1958	10.5	1971	10.3
1959	10.6	1972	10.1
1960	10.8	1973	9.9
1961	10.2	1974	8.7
1962	10.0	1975	8.4
		1976	8.6

Source: Annual Abstracts of Statistics, HMSO.

expenditure in the first years of the NHS the proportion of total costs absorbed by drugs remained consistently around the 10–11 per cent level for over two decades. By 1973, however, this percentage began to fall and by 1975 it had returned to its 1950 level of 8.4 per cent. Moreover, as Fig. 4.2 illustrates this fairly consistent proportion of total NHS expenditure was accompanied by a rise in the number of prescriptions written, from 223.8 million in 1949 to 346.2 million in 1975.

Soon after Hinchcliffe reported two main events ensured that the industry's pricing levels and practices remained in the front of British political debate. One was the publicity given in the UK to the Kefauver Committee's investigations[6] in the USA. The other was the widely reported disagreement and ultimate legal battle between the American drug firm Pfizer and the NHS over the price to be paid for the antibiotic Terramycin.

Kefauver examined individual products and named several which were showing a profit margin at selling price of more than 90 per cent over factory costs.[7] Findings of this nature were presented or summarised both in British academic journals and in popularly distributed books.[8]

In the UK itself similar, apparently dramatic price and profit levels

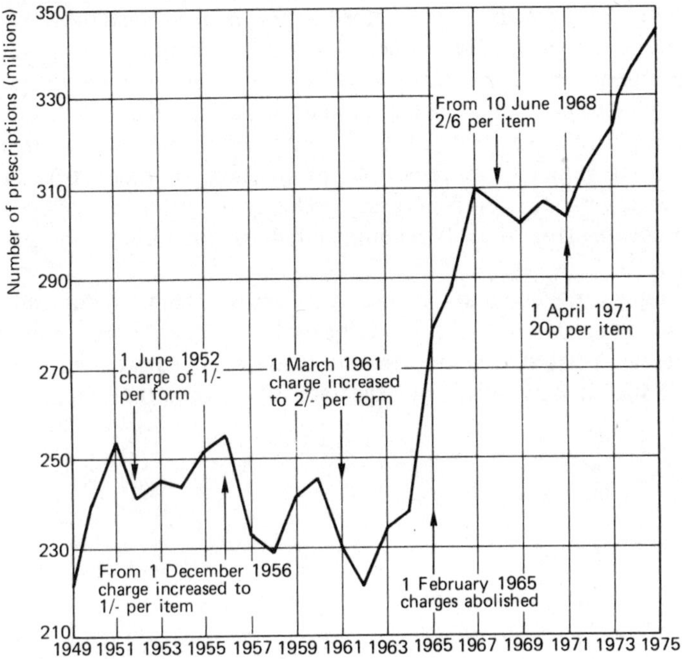

Fig. 4.2. Number of prescriptions in United Kingdom (1949–74).
Source: Office of Health Economics, *op. cit.*

were revealed when DDSA Pharmaceuticals Ltd. offered to supply tetracycline to the NHS for £6 — 10*s* per 1000 tablets. Pfizer, who held the patent on the product, had at that time (1961) as selling price of £60 for the same volume of tablets. In an attempt to force Pfizer to reduce its price the Minister of Health, Enoch Powell, authorised the importation of tetracycline for use in the hospital services of the NHS. The importers were not licensed to sell the drug by Pfizer who challenged their right to supply the product. The Minister justified the legality of his action by claiming that the hospital services were Crown users. The House of Lords upheld the Minister's claim by a 3:2 majority verdict. As a 'Crown user' the Minister invoked Section 46 of the 1949 Patents Act. This section permitted any goverment department, or person authorised by the same, to work any patent 'for the services of the Crown'. Thc patentee could, and in Pfizer's case did, claim compensation for breach of his protected status.

These examples and others helped to perpetuate offical unease about the industry's profits and prices. A further committee, the Sainsbury Committee, was consequently set up and reported in 1967. The Sainsbury Report[9] examined a number of the variables which affect or are alleged to affect price-levels. It confirmed the earlier finding made by the Hinchliffe Committee that proprietary or branded medicines where taking an ever-increasing share of total pharmaceutical expenditures (Fig. 4.3). It recommended the total abolition of brand names.[20]

Whatever the economic merits or demerits of that recommendation the trend depicted in Fig. 4.3. was inevitable. It is hard to remember that the research-based drug industry barely existed in its present form until the 1940s. It was only from the late 1940s that the specific active

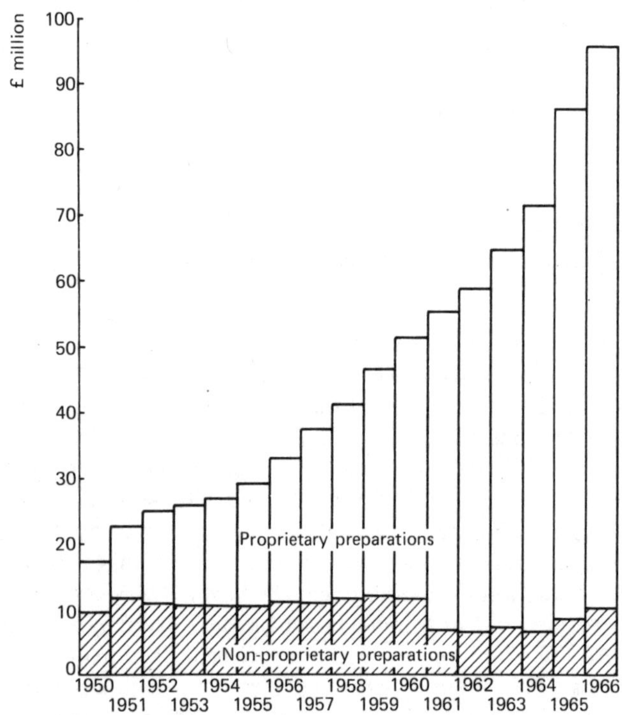

Fig. 4.3. The cost of proprietary and non-proprietary preparations prescribed in the general medical and pharmaceutical services. England and Wales (1950–66).

Source: Sainsbury, *op. cit.*, p. 23.

chemical ingredients for a new generation of medicines started to emerge from the industrial pharmaceutical research laboratories. Given that the majority of these medicines were mostly patented and so company specific, their possession of a brand name was of little economic importance in the short run. In the longer run, after patent expiry, arguments such as those Sainsbury deployed could be used to support the prohibition of branding. Nevertheless, no specific government action has been taken on this issue.

The Sainsbury Committee also recommended a revision of the Voluntary Price Regulation Scheme (VPRS) which the industry had agreed with the British Government and which had existed in one form or another since 1957. It went on to comment[11] 'that, since the negotiation of prices may sometimes fail to result in agreement; *a procedure must be available* (emphasis added) to which Ministers may have resource'. The VPRS was subsequently amended. The specific Sainsbury recommendation that Section 46 of the 1949 Patents Act be widened to embrace not only the hospital services, but also the much larger drug market of the General Medical and Pharmaceutical Services, was adopted. In 1968 the Health Services and Public Health Act extended the 'services of the Crown' provision to include explicitly the prescription of drugs by GPs. Moreover, the Banks Committee,[12] which reported two years later in 1969, proposed reforms of the earlier patent system and recommended that Section 46 be retained as a 'sanction' if the Department of Health was of the opinion that a patentee's prices were too high.

Government price-control of pharmaceuticals commenced in the UK in 1957 under the auspices of the VPRS. In 1977 the scheme's name was amended to the Pharmaceutical Price Regulation Scheme (PPRS), reflecting more correctly that lack of voluntarism which existed given the 'sanctions' and 'procedures' of last 'recourse' which Ministers have available under Section 46.[13]

The Scheme has been revised several times over the last 20 years; it is not statutory and consequently can be reorganised if conditions change. Basically, the PPRS provides a framework for negotiation between the Department of Health and Social Security (DHSS) and the firm marketing a medicine. All companies with NHS sales of over £0.75 million must supply the DHSS with a standardised Annual Financial Return (AFR) which gives details of sales, costs and capital employed in the previous year. The DHSS thus has at its disposal information on promotion levels and profitability.

In the course of negotiation firms may be called upon to satisfy the Department on other matters, including transfer prices of materials supplied by affiliated companies, and the amount of overseas costs and capital, including R & D expenditure, to be taken into account in considering the firm's UK business.

The AFR is provided retrospectively within six months of the end of the firm's accounting year. The view of the DHSS is that it is fair for the NHS to accept the cost of R & D *pro rata* to its share of a firm's global business.[14] Sales promotional expenses are allowable as a cost in PPRS negotiations. In 1976 these amounted to 14 per cent of NHS sales for the industry as a whole. By 1979 the DHSS intends only to accept 10 per cent of total sales as an allowable cost, albeit promotion expenditure above the figure will not be banned.

Despite its name, the PPRS aims to control profits, rather than prices. The DHSS 'think that it is unrealistic to allocate all of a company's costs ... between the different medicines it supplies'.[15] Instead the Department prefers to look at a firm's overall return on capital 'on the assumption that if that is reasonable, what the NHS pays for the totality of supplies ... will also be reasonable.'

'Reasonableness', of course, is a concept with no generally accepted meaning. The DHSS accept this and regard a level of profitability which would be common to all firms at all times as 'quite impracticable and certainly undersirable'.[16] Nevertheless, the DHSS must work within the general guidelines laid down to all Departmental purchasers, namely that '*suppliers of goods to Government must earn the same sort of profits as British industry in general*'[17] (emphasis added).

Under the PPRS, if historic profitability is regarded as too low (or too high) by one party to the negotiation then it will try to raise (or lower) prices. In addition to the historic AFR, firms also submit forecast AFRs within a three-month period prior to the year in question. And if they wish to request an across-the-board price rise, they will also be asked for an AFR for the current year based on current prices so that a forecast of the adequacy or otherwise of profitability can be made on the assumption that the additional revenue is not forthcoming.

PRICE: MARGINAL COST RATIO AS A RATIONALE FOR PRICE CONTROL

To the economist 'reasonableness' or 'adequacy' of profit is not so difficult to define at least in principle, as it is to the layman. 'Reasonable' profits exist when they are sufficiently large to call forth the resources to produce the goods and services which consumers want in the quantities and qualities they prefer and at the prices they are prepared to pay. Profits above or below this level are unreasonable or inadequate. In addition the level will vary industry by industry and period by period according to varying conditions of tastes, preferences, demand, innovation and technology, and risk and uncertainty.

It is difficult to understand, therefore, how the PPRS can possibly be operated in such a way that inter-industry and inter-temporal differences of this sort can be taken into account while still operating within the general government guidelines of moving drug industry profits up or down towards the British industrial average. Drug profits will probably emerge at a level above or below what the economist (and so the consumer in the market place) considers adequate. In consequence an excess or a deficiency of productive resources will flow into pharmaceuticals. The resource-attracting magnetism of drug profits will be greater or less than that which the market would prefer except in the unlikely event that drug profits 'should' be close to British industrial average profitability levels.

Presumably the rationale for the existence of a price control scheme such as the PPRS is the belief that unregulated market forces are failing to bring about price-levels which would result in reasonable profits in drugs. This belief may exist because on the demand side of the market doctors and patients do not pay directly for the medicines they prescribe and consume and are indifferent to the prices paid by the NHS; or it may be because on the supply side firms are believed to have the ability persistently to price their products above reasonable levels since competitive market rivalry is absent, for whatever reason.

If the case for price control in the industry is indeed rational then it is based on the presence of some form of monopoly power derived from one of these sources. In the former instance, demand elasticity (or price sensitivity) could be an appropriate measure of monopoly power. In the latter, monopoly could be measured by the number of firms in the industry or by its concentration ratio. By these criteria the pharmaceutical industry would be regarded as relatively competitive.[18] However, numbers of firms and concentration ratios are at best poor proxies as yardsticks of monopoly power. Ease of industry entry is probably more important. If an industry is earning profits of an unreasonable level and if entry barriers are absent, then new firms will come into that industry and, in order to gain sales, will price at levels below the ruling rate. In the long run this will reduce both prices and profits to normal, competitive levels.[19]

This emphasis on the competitive process itself and on the level of price, *vis à vis* market structure, has been recognised by industrial economists. The condition of price above marginal cost leads to 'an allocation of resources which is inefficient in the sense of satisfying consumer wants with less than maximum effectiveness'. It is this (P > MC), not the number or size of firms, which is the 'basis of the economist's most general condemnation of monopoly'.[20] Moreover, studies of market structure tell us nothing of the impact on industry pricing of doctor or patient price-conciousness. Examinations of P:MC ratios and demand elasticity, on the other hand, do so. They also provide a criterion by which the industry's pricing behaviour can be assessed and reasons why the observed behaviour takes the pattern it does.

In the remainder of this chapter we review several studies of competition in the drug industry in both the UK and the USA. They show how, over the years, a better understanding of price:marginal cost ratios has developed. Both 'price' and 'marginal cost' are terms which can be difficult to comprehend. They have different meanings in the short and in the long run. The inferences to be drawn from static or dynamic studies of the two can vary widely. In the next chapter an international comparison is made of recent studies carried out by Reekie in the highly regulated UK market and in the relatively non-regulated US market. The implications of this comparison for future price regulation in both countries concludes our discussion on price.

EARLY STUDIES OF PRICING BEHAVIOUR

The problem of how properly to define price and marginal cost lies at the heart of the debate surrounding drug industry pricing. In the first studies made of the industry's pricing practices price was usually described as money price per capsule, thousand capsules, pills, tablets or whatever. Marginal cost was defined as the cost of producing one extra unit of the product in question, 'unit' referring to the physical form and volume to which the price was ascribed.

Henry Steele[21] and W. S. Comanor[22] were two of the earliest academic economists to examine price competition in the drug industry. Both relied heavily on data and inferences drawn from the Kefauver Report.[23] Kefauver, for example, cited several illustrations where money price was well above marginal cost. One such was prednisolone. Bulk prednisolone was available on the open market 'to all comers', and if a tableting and bottling charge was added the cost of the finished product was 1.5 cents per pill. The Schering Corporation was discovered, however, to be selling prednisolone, an antiarthritic drug, to the pharmacist at 17.9 cents per tablet and to the consumer at 30 cents.[24] Data of this sort are impressive. Kefauver argued that 'no more dramatic illustration of the effect of monopoly on the consumer can be found than in the drug industry'.[25]

Both Comanor and Steele agreed with the view that the industry was not competitive. But Comanor took the position that it was only *after* the beginning of what is now called the 'therapeutic revolution' that the industry began to move away from a perfectly competitive position. In reference to the unpatented drugs penicillin and streptomycin he stated that it 'may well be that (their prices) fell to the vicinity of short run marginal cost'.[26] In order to avoid a repetition of this Comanor argued that 'it was clear (to firms) . . . that profits in the future would depend on the development of more protected market positions'.[27] Product differentiation, achieved by advertising and research and development would, he argued, 'provide the producer with substantial control over the prices of his products as well as act as a significant barrier to entry into the relevant therapeutic market'.[28]

Using similar data from the Kefauver Report, Steele came to the same basic conclusions. The industry's 'response to the given economic framework . . . (has been) to exploit the monopolistic potential inherent in trademarks, the patent privilege, and the great inelasticity of market demand, in such a way as to overcome the potential for competition . . .'[29] Comanor concluded that in consequence '(a) high degree of price stability on existing products has been maintained'.[30] While Steele deduced that 'the ethical drug industry might be highly competitive, perhaps almost purely competitive in the absence of patent protection' and brand names.[31]

Studies of drug-industry pricing in the UK lagged behind the US ones reported on above but were generally carried out in a similar theoretical and empirical framework. Even as recently as 1973 the Monopolies Commission in its Report[32] on Roche Products, the British end of the Swiss multinational Hoffman–La Roche, revealed that in 1970 the Swiss parent was charging its British subsidiary £370 and £922 per kilo for the ingredients of Librium and Valium respectively. These same ingredients were simultaneously available from other manufacturers at £9 and £20 in Italy. The Commission notionally adjusted the firm's international transfer prices in the light of this information, recalculated the firm's financial accounts and pronounced that the profits made by Roche were 'quite unjustified' and were the direct result of 'excessive prices charged'. The company was ordered to cut the 1970 prices of its two main products, Librium and Valium, by 60 per cent and by 75 per cent respectively. Again simple monetary price was being contrasted with short-run marginal cost and conclusions were drawn. The earlier and broader-ranging Sainsbury Committee,[33] spoke of 'what is commonly understood' as price competition. This is derived from the kind of competition described in economic testbooks as 'perfect competition'. This abstract model defines conditions in a market with many small sellers of a homogeneous product where no one has the power to influence price because the amount each supplies is small in relation to the total market. 'Price competition' in such circumstances takes the form of passive acceptance by each supplier of the ruling market price, which will be the lowest price consistent with minimum profit and which he cannot exceed without sacrificing all his sales to competing suppliers.

This would appear to be an ideal situation in forcing down prices to no more than minimum cost (incorporating minimum profit), and in this sense it constitutes 'perfect competition'. In contrast, a situation like that of the pharmaceutical industry, with only a few major suppliers and where each is conscious of possible retaliation from his rivals if he cuts his price, is seen as non-ideal. Price-cutting is restrained by fear of retaliation, while branding and sales promotion are seen as wasteful because they would not be needed if competing suppliers' products were indistinguishable from one another.

In practice, this theoretically 'perfect' model is not only unrealistic as a description of the real world, but is far from ideal as a prescription for what ought to exist. Perhaps in a zeal for mathematical tidiness, or because the theory concentrated unduly on the very rare cases of 'atomistic' industries of the type it described, the theoretical ideal of perfect competition entirely omitted the dimension of quality — and the related possibility of innovation which makes 'quality' (in the widest sense including performance of the product) subject to improvement.

The pervasiveness of the phrase 'perfect competition' and the price: short run marginal cost ratios discovered in Pfizer's terramycin case and in Roche's Librium–Valium cases, however, have led to what might be termed the 'British received view'. This view is summarised, with little risk of parody, in the following paragraphs.

Medicines are a necessity and, as such, an increase in price will drive few people from the market, neither will a decrease attract many into it. This necessity effect which results in demand inelasticity is reinforced by the fact that the actual selection of the product is made by a third party — the doctor — not the patient or final consumer and, at least in the UK, payment is made by a fourth party to the transaction, the NHS. Cooper[34] has stated that 'demand responds to the incidence of sickness, the quality of therapy available to treat it, and to sales promotion, but very little else'. In other words, the industry may be close to the Galbraithian situation where the firm 'controls the prices at which it sells and takes steps to insure that the public, other producers, or the state take the planned quantities at these prices'.[35]

Secondly, the firms adjust their prices according to the actions of those rivals whose products are close substitutes. In pharmaceuticals this condition exists within the highly concentrated therapeutic sub-markets, between which cross-elasticity of demand is low. In accordance with at least some oligopoly theories, price competition should therefore, not be expected. Prices will tend to be rigid, and that at a high level. Comanor[36] adheres to this view and suggests that the consequent existence of monopoly profits reduces the pressures on drug firms to lower costs. Lower costs, he argues, could permit the charging of lower prices but, given inelastic demand and oligopolisitic uncertainties, this would not lead to sufficiently attractive increases in revenues. The use of price as an important competitive tool is, consequently, unlikely.

Thirdly, the prices of existing pharmaceutical products are allegedly rarely altered[37] and when product duplication occurs price equivalence is frequently the case.[38]

The Monopolies Commission[39], in a general report, state that they view the first two of these points (inelastic demand and high concentration levels) as necessary (although not sufficient) conditions from which to predict the probable absence of price competition in an industry. In which case the third point (stable, parallel prices) might be deduced by the Commission to be the outcome of collusive, monopolisitic price leadership and not that of competitive forces.

The Sainsbury Committee[40] explicitly concluded that they 'did not gain the impression that there was any significant degree of price competition in medical specialty products'. This conclusion was arrived at after the Committee had surveyed and asked how prices were determined. Some said they considered the prices of alternatives, others that they aimed to obtain a required rate of return on investment and others that they tried to recover cost in a given period. These objectives need not be incompatible, but the latter two in particular could appear to depend on rule-of-thumb pricing tools. Many writers have argued persuasively that the use of such rules helps to eliminate oligopolistic uncertainties and increases industry discipline in loose-knit cartels[41].

Although restricted to a specific case, the outcome of Roche Products' disagreement with the British government may give some indication of how official views in the UK are changing with regard to both the meaning of 'competition' and to the inferences to be drawn from ratios of price over short-run marginal cost. Between 1973 and 1976 the firm engaged in a heated and costly battle with the Government. The controversy covered many issues. But in essence Roche's case was that they were prepared to negotiate prices with the government through the official VPRS or to accept a weakening of their patent rights so as to permit other firms to manufacture identical products and thus have prices regulated by competition; but not both.

When the government permitted two other firms to market Librium and Valium equivalents by invoking a little-used section of the Patents Acts,[42] Roche withdrew from the VPRS negotiations and were referred to the Monopolies Commission. Succeeding price reductions by Roche in the six months after the launch of the rival products amounted to 36 per cent on Valium alone. This was dismissed by the commission not as competitive reaction but as misjudgment of 'the strength of the competition'.

On 12 November 1975 Mrs Shirley Williams, Secretary of State for Prices and Consumer Protection, announced to the Commons that an agreement had been reached whereby the company would repay £12 million of 'excessive profits' to the government in respect of the period January 1970 to April 1973. Her statement concluded that 'this sort of settlement should be regarded by any company attempting to make high profits as a suitable indication of what might happen.'[43]

On closer inspection, however, the agreement may reveal a remarkable change of stance by the government. First, Roche was immediately permitted to raise the prices of Librium and Valium by 50 per cent and 100 per cent respectively. Second, the government refused to disclose to what level the Valium price would have risen under the normal VPRS rules. Certainly Roche wished for more than a 100 per cent increase. This was an implicit admission by the government that the price should have been more than doubled but that politically this would have been unacceptable. Certainly, the new average daily dosage cost per patient of 1.04p for 10 mgs. (previously 0.52p) could hardly be regarded as high in absolute terms and, relatively, it was still lower than that charged in many overseas countries. Moreover, in April 1976 Valium's agreed price was allowed to rise a further 45 per cent.[44]

Third, Roche rejoined the VPRS, from which they had been excluded since their selfimposed withdrawal. This permitted them to raise the prices of their other products and, presumably, build in a premium for any restriction on the Valium increase. Fourth, the government repaid Roche £8.25 million as a consequence of profits forgone by the company in the 2½ years during which the price-cutting order was in force. The government thus explicitly conceded that the price reductions it ordered were too severe and so in tangible terms the Roche payment to the government shrank from £12 million to a net £3.75 million.

Fifthly, given that Roche are a Swiss multinational company with an ability to manipulate international monetary flows to their own best advantage, this 'penalty' shrank still further. Roche no doubt used Swiss francs to buy sterling to pay the government. The pound, however, depreciated by approximately 30 per cent against the franc between the dates the profits were earned and (presumably) remitted back to Basel at the then ruling rates of exchange. The cost to Hoffman–La Roche was consequently around one-third less than the £3.75 million in terms of currencies (e.g. francs or dollars) other than sterling.

Finally, if due account is taken of the time value of money (by discounting and compounding where appropriate) then the real economic penalty suffered by the company is still further reduced. (The profits were earned in years prior to 1970 and not repaid till 1976.)

It would be facile to assume that the government was unaware of all this. More realistically, it seems that it heeded the advice of the chemical industry's 'little Neddy', or EDC, which pointed out that the British drug industry's prices were not only relatively low by international standards, but were drifting lower owing to continuous governmental pressures. According to the National Economic Development Office, if that state of affairs continued, then 'both the incentive to invest in the UK and the supply of necessary funds would be reduced'.[45] This is not strictly true, as Roche's continuing expansion of research and development facilities in the UK during the last year or so has shown. Again, however, this was largely due to Roche being able to fund expansion from profits earned world-wide.

Britain is an attractive location for investment by multinational pharmaceutical firms because of its highly regarded medical establishment, a speedy system of drug registration, the English language, a satisfactory patent system, political stability, and last (but by no means least) low wage and salary costs. On the other hand, many foreign nations use British drug prices as a yardstick against which to measure their own prices when negotiating with pharmaceutical firms. To the extent that this is so, then the NEDO prediction could become self-fulfilling and the firms who would be hardest hit would be the British domiciled firms, which depend heavily on sales in the UK and Commonwealth.

Why has this remarkable improvement taken place in the relationship between industry and government? Possibly the reason lies in the fact that more and more modern medicines have lower and lower volumes of active ingredient per dosage unit and that this phenomenon has now been acknowledged by government negotiators.[46] The consequence of this is that the overheads (research and development and the like), which must be recouped by the innovating firm, will form an ever increasing proportion of the transfer price per kilo but a decreasing proportion of the price per unit dose. This is illustrated in Table 4.2.

Given that the market for pharmaceutical products is measured by morbidity rates and so by comparative dosage units—not by comparative weights of active substance — this trend will produce ever-more apparently outrageous differences between the transfer prices of international research-based firms and the simple production cost-

Table 4.2. Overheads as a proportion of transfer price for two hypothetical pharmaceuticals, A and B

	Active substance compound A	Active substance compound B
Transfer price per kilo from parent to British subsidiary	£300	£3,000
Production cost	£100	£ 100
Contribution per kilo to parent's overheads (e.g. research) and profit	£200	£2,900
Active substance per capsule or dosage unit	500 mg	5 mg
Contribution to parent per 2,000 dosage units	£200	£29

Source: Q. H. Novotny, *The Economics of the Pharmaceutical Industry*, Henry Durant Institute (Geneva, 1974)

Table 4.3. Transfer price in relation to production cost: an escalating ratio

(1) Production cost of active Substance	(2) R & D and other contributions to parent %	(3) Transfer price (1) + (2) %	(4) Multiple (3)/(1)
16% –eg 500 mg	33	49	3
3% –eg 50 mg	33	36	12
1% –eg 25 mg	33	34	34
0.3% –eg 5 mg	33	33.3	100
0.1% –eg 1 mg	33	33.1	331

As percentage of selling price of finished product

Source: Novotny, *op. cit.*

related prices of imitating firms. The Valium transfer price was 50 times as great as the potential purchase price from an Italian imitator. This multiple could easily have been many times higher and with future drugs it may well be — as the hypothetical figures in Table 4.3 indicate. In theory, the multiple could rise to infinity with no implications of either excessive or deficient profits.

Monetary prices for drugs are very high in relation to short-run marginal costs. As a consequence the industry has been condemned for noncompetitive pricing behaviour in both the USA and UK. In the UK two firms, Pfizer and Roche, have been explicitly penalised. In addition the entire British industry is subject to the PPRS price-control scheme. It is not improbable that price:marginal cost ratios will rise still further. Overhead costs, in particular R & D, continue to rise. Short-run variable costs, however, may well be diminishing per unit of output. These considerations make it likely that the ostensible rationale for price control in the industry will be strengthened. The theories discussed next pose the question as to whether perfect competition and the price:short-run marginal cost ratio are the appropriate criteria from which to adduce the presence of optimal resource allocation.

LATER THEORIES OF PRICE AND MARGINAL COST

In recent years a new body of literature has been emerging. This has attempted to shift the study of drug-industry pricing away from attempts to fit or explain that behaviour within the framework of atomistic perfect competition. Instead, attempts have been made to develop dynamic theories of oligopolistic competition which could be used to predict and explain pricing patterns in drugs. From these newer theories it has been hoped that welfare inferences can be drawn.

George and Priscilla Polanyi[47] argue that standard microeconomic theory is guilty of both unjustifiable generalisations and over-simplification in its approach to price. Real world competition is not 'perfect'. A multiplicity of suppliers and consumers do not deal with each other in homogeneous products, nor in the absence of ignorance, in the presence of costless factor mobility, with no economics of scale and so on. Rather, the alternative model of oligopolistic competition is applicable to pharmaceuticals. The assumptions, processes and outcomes of that model are less determinate than under 'perfectly' competitive conditions, but they are both more realistic and more satisfactory from the point of view of consumer welfare. There, account is taken of differences in the quality and performance of the product and in the service given by the supplier (reliable delivery, constant dependable standard in product and service, technical advice), and the concept of price competition is radically extended. It now becomes 'price plus product' competition. Suppliers compete by offering rival packages of 'price plus product quality' and the customer chooses between them according to relative advantage from the merits of the product and relative cost represented by their price.

This is the kind of competition, say the Polanyis, which now exists in pharmaceuticals as in many other sectors of manufacturing industry. It adds an extra dimension, both to the scope of competition and to the range of customer satisfactions which the competition provides. It creates the contemporary world of vastly improved and ever-improving products. This has replaced the era of largely standardised and uniform products with little tendency to improve (for example in the early stages in the cotton industry), which characterised the first period of industrialisation in Britain and provided the model for the textbook ideal of 'perfect' price competition.

If we accept that this is the new form of price competition and that it has clearly brought benefits — of which the therapeutic revolution in drugs is one example — that are not to be cast aside by turning the clock back to the era of uniform and largely unchanging products, the consequences of this new form of competition must also be accepted. First, if the supplier is to have an incentive to offer a better product (and this must include the possibility of offering the same product but with his own assurance of reliability in service, quality, etc.) he must have the right to sell it as a distinctive, identifiable (*i.e.*, branded) product. Unless this right is available we are back in the era of undistinguishable products, where no improvement or innovation can bring extra profits exclusively to the supplier. If he cannot reap the rewards there is no incentive to make improvements. Hence the observation made long ago by Schumpeter that 'perfect' price competition (or price equal to short run marginal cost) is a prescription for the nonexistence of innovation.[48]

None of this discussion, of course, is novel. But 'perfect' competition, either because of its analytic elegance or the connotation of the adjective, is a concept which continues to attract economists and policy-makers as a relevant yardstick by which to gauge industrial performance.

Professor J. F. Weston[49] emphasises how necessary it is to move away from simplistic, static, *ceteris paribus* theories to a long-run dynamic framework. Pricing decisions, he argues, are made in a complex, interdependent environment:

> Broad environmental influences, combined with the constraints presented by existing products and firms in the market, lead the firm to develop adaptive policies with respect to product, quality, prices, sales methods, promotion efforts, service organization and financial facilities. These decisions, in turn, have an influence on the quantity and type of fixed investments and on the level and behaviour of other costs. Even on new products, constraints are set by the market, since new products substitute in some degree for older products . . . Iterated reviews of product quality characteristics, materials characteristics, production methods, and marketing methods seek the optimal product quality, cost levels and marketing attractiveness . . . (A)dministrative discretion is exercised in selecting among alternative combinations of choices under uncertainty involving pricing decisions in relation to the other variables . . . The combination of broad environmental influences and the constraints presented by existing products and firms in the market have an impact on the range of policies adopted by the firm with respect to product quality, prices, sales methods, promotion efforts, service organization and financial facilities. These decisions, in turn, have an influence on the quantity and types of fixed investments. These also have an influence on the (possible chosen) level(s) and behaviour of other costs. This produces a range of expected volumes or turnover

of investment. These . . . can be expected to result in responses by other firms in the industry. By relating the expected level and behaviour of costs to expected prices and volume in relationships to the total investment involved, an expected return on investment is indicated.

A large number of uncertainties are involved at each place in the decision process. There are uncertainties with regard to both the present and future behaviour of rivals. The elements of the broader environmental factors are also subject to change. As a consequence, there are capital investment decisions involving probability distributions and uncertainty at each stage of the process.

Therefore the analysis may be repeated with alternate judgements about the probabilities involved. This may yield another expected return on investment. By repeating the process, probability distributions of returns on investment will result. The decision-makers in the firm will accept the investment or reject it depending on the level of the expected returns and the degree of dispersion in the probability distribution and particularly the cumulated probability that the investment might earn below a required return on investment.

Table 4.4. Weston's summary of factors influencing drug prices

A. *Demand*

1. Product characteristics defined by (*a*) acceptability, (*b*) efficacy, and (*c*) absence of side effects.
2. The therapeutic qualities of a drug in relation to other products.
3. Classes of physicians who are the most likely prescribers.
4. Price schedules for related products.
5. Daily dosage quantity and expected duration of patient therapy.
6. Dosage or treatment costs in a health care program.
7. Effects on related costs in a health care program.
8. Extent and characteristics of probable users, considering age group, income levels, etc.
9. Elasticity of demand with respect to price.
10. Cross elasticities of demand with respect to price and product qualities.
11. Elasticity of demand with respect to income.
12. Probability and timing of appearance of new competing products.
13. Projected volume at various prices.
14. Duration and pattern of probable product life-cycle.
15. Extent of use of prepayment plans, insurance plans, and government programs in paying for health care and drugs.

Table 4.4. (continued)

B. *Supply*
1. Number and types of competing products.
2. Number and types of competing companies.
3. Rate of future prospective development of competing products.
4. Research, production and quality control requirements expressed in required investments and cost levels.
5. Nature of distribution systems required for effective marketing.
6. Size, forms and strengths of products to be marketed.
7. Expected shelf-life of products.
8. Patent position of the firm in relation to other products and firms.
9. Other products produced by the firm and their prospective prices, costs, volume and returns.
10. Ease of imitation or improvements by others.
11. Location of production in relation to markets served; domestic vs exports.
12. Sources of raw materials.
13. Differences in required associated services to the medical profession.
14. Tax patterns.
15. Government regulations and procedures required for certifying drugs.
16. Sources and costs of capital
17. Types of scientific and technical capabilities required.
18. Production and quality-control supervision by regulatory agencies.

C. *General Environment*
1. Size of the economy.
2. Percentage of income spent on health care.
3. Nature and expectations toward health care systems.
4. Consumption habits and patterns with respect to the use of pharmaceuticals.
5. Standard of living in the economy.
6. Size and distribution of gross national product.
7. Characteristics of the political environment.
8. Role of government in payment for health care.
9. Role of government as regulator and inspector.
10. Rate of growth of the economy.
11. Economic instability or stability.
12. Patterns of price changes in the economy as a whole.
13. Import, export, foreign exchange regulations.
14. Antidumping regulations.
15. Laws with respect to patents.
16. Laws and administrative policies with respect to compulsory licensing.
17. Licensing regulations.
18. Comparative licensing regulations among different countries.

Finally, Weston uses the foregoing framework to reconsider a generalisation with respect to oligopoly theory, or what we have specifically renamed the 'British received view' of drug pricing.[50] This relates to the proposition that oligopolistic awareness will lead to spontaneous collusion. Weston argues that this concept of oligopolistic awareness is only plausible in the setting of partial equilibrium analysis. If decision-making is limited to output or pricing so that there was only one dimension of interaction, oligopolistic awareness would indeed be facilitated. But he says:

> The reality is great complexity in the decision-making process involving output or pricing decisions. There are a large number of interacting areas, each with numerous vectors. These areas include research and development, product variations, quality of product, style of product, manufacturing processes, management techniques, channels of distribution, advertising methods, etc. The dimensions of decision making in the business firm are much too complex, with too many dimensions to permit oligopolistic awareness to have any realistic meaning.[51]

Table 4.4 summarises Weston's discussion on the multiplicity of demand, supply and environmental factors which can influence pharmaceutical price. Prices of all products are multi-dimensional. In drugs, Weston argues, the main dimensions are the following:

Quality = (1) Efficacy + (2) safety +
(3) Clinical evidence + experience +
(4) Information communicated to doctors and other professionals +
(5) Reputation of manufacturer based on performance of prior products

Nominal price = price to wholesaler less discounts to wholesaler less discounts and rebates to hospital or other distribution outlets.

(Actual) price = (nominal price) ÷ quality

In analysing the behaviour of prices and the price responsiveness of quantity sold to apparent price changes, it is quality-adjusted prices that need to be taken into account in the analysis and not just the nominal price. This view will be developed further in the empirical work reported on in the next chapter. In the meantime we will transfer our attention from the definition of price to that of marginal cost.

Mark Schankerman[52] recently articulated the problems which face regulators if they attempt to set product price equal to marginal cost. The problems are particularly acute when there is a relatively large amount of non-allocable common or joint costs which must be recouped from the market but which cannot be attributed to any particular product. (For example, basic pharmaceutical R & D conducted prior to the emergence of a product candidate, and developmental pharmaceutical R & D carried out on candidates which fail to reach the market or, if they do, which fail in turn to be commercial successes.) Schankerman calculated that anything between 81 and 91 per cent of total pharmaceutical R & D outlay falls into the common-cost category, depending on the share of R & D expected prior to candidate emergence and on the minimal success ratio of product candidates on which R & D effort is laid out. His results are shown in Table 4.5.

Table 4.5. Schankerman's estimates of common costs in R & D

Annual research expenditures as a fraction of annual development costs for product candidates initiated	Terminal success ratio	
	0.09	0.17
0.2	0.89	0.81
0.3	0.90	0.82
0.4	0.90	0.83
0.5	0.91	0.84

Source: Schankerman, *op. cit.*, p. 8

The basic problem is that the price of a drug must exceed its marginal cost of production in order to contain its own assignable overhead costs and also that portion of common costs allocated to it, both apportioned over the quantity of the product sold. How great should this excess be? And how should it vary drug by drug?

Given that all products should be priced at long-run marginal cost, common costs should be allocated in such a way as to minimise the social losses which arise due to the resulting prices and so reduced consumption. In discrete terms this will be achieved when the following relationship holds between any two commodities:

$$\frac{MSB_1}{DWL_1} = \frac{MSB_2}{DWL_2} \qquad (1)$$

where the subscripts denote the products, and *MSB* and *DWL* respectively indicate the social benefits obtained by the marginal consumer and the deadweight loss incurred as a consequence of the relevant common costs being added to the perfectly competitive price of each product. The equality can be rewritten as:

$$\frac{Z_1}{Z_2} = \frac{DWL_1}{DWL_2} \qquad (2)$$

where *Z* denotes the price-production cost mark-up for each product. That is $Z \; \Delta P/P$ where ΔP is the mark-up required to cover pro-rated common costs, and *P* is the original perfectly competive price, $P = MC$. Optimality then, occurs when the social benefits from all products as measured by the market's willingness to pay the price premium are equal at the margin per pound of deadweight loss necessarily forgone to cover common costs. (Subject to the constraint that total incremental revenue, $\sum_{i=1}^{2} R_i$, is constant and equal to common costs.)

The implications of this relationship can be intuitively understood by reference to Fig. 4.4a, which is similar to that used by Schankerman.[53] Products 1 and 2 have demand curves D_1D_1 and D_2D_2 respectively. In both cases marginal production costs equal *MC*. If the share of common costs allocated to each product is the same then *MC* rises to MC^1 and the original competitive levels of $X_1^* = X_2^*$ fall to X_1 and X_2. The respective deadweight losses are given by the shaded and the dotted region. It is clear that minimisation of the aggregate deadweight losses implies that products with a relatively price-elastic demand should bear a relatively smaller share of common costs than those with an inelastic demand, other things equal.

Prices should be set in such a way that the proportionate change in output from the original competitive levels should be the same for all products, irrespective of market size. This can be shown diagrammatically at the expense only of some generalisation. Figure 4.4b is restricted to the same two-product case, and equivalent competitive output levels of $x_1^* = x_2^*$ and *MC* levels of $P_1 = P_2$ assumed.

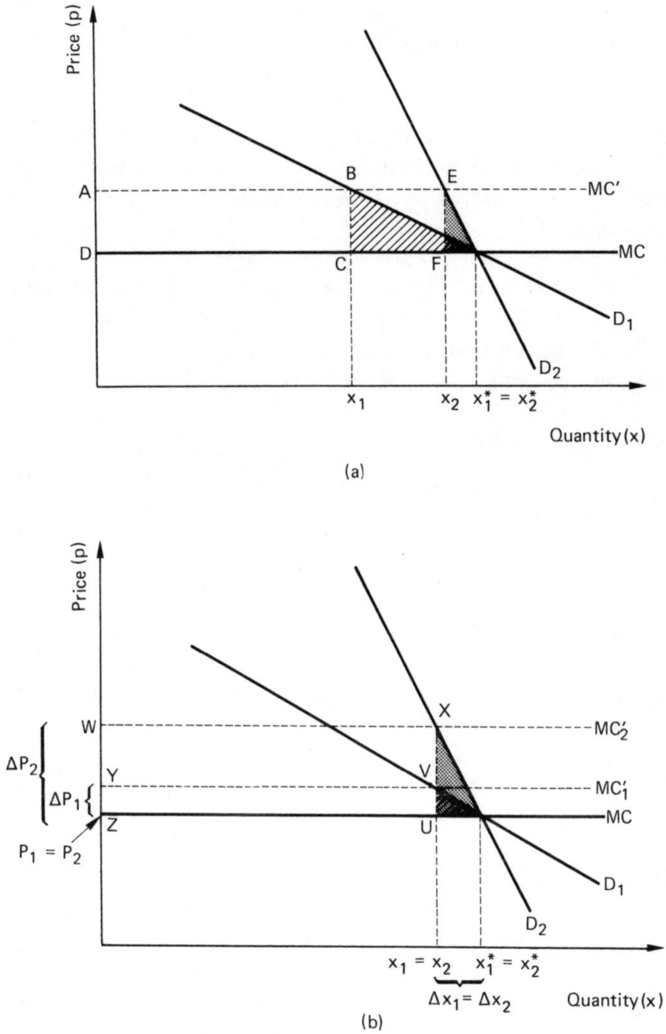

Fig. 4.4. Demand curves for drugs with differing price elasticities. (Prices set to reflect differing mark-ups.)
Note: Prices are set so that:

$$ABCD + AEFD = WXUZ + YVUZ$$

i.e. so that total incremental revenue equals common costs.

Total incremental revenue required to cover common costs, $\sum_{i=1}^{2} R_i$, is $ABCD + AEFD$ (as indicated in Fig. 4.4a). In the optimal situation $\sum_{i=1}^{2} R_i$ must be constant and equation (1) satisfied. Thus $ABCD + AEFD$ must equal $WXUZ + YVUZ$ in Fig. 4.4b. Clearly the sum of the deadweight losses (the dotted plus the shaded triangles) is less in Fig. 4.4b. No other pricing policy would result in a smaller aggregate deadweight loss.

It can readily be inferred that the optimal allocation of common costs is such that P_1 and P_2 should be raised ΔP_1 and ΔP_2 respectively, and output should be reduced by the equal proportions $\Delta X_1 = \Delta X_2$. To prove this, assume that the price elevations are sufficiently small so that elasticities are constant over the relevant range. Then:

$$DWL_1 = \tfrac{1}{2}\Delta P_1 \Delta X_1 \tag{3}$$

But elasticity of demand for product 1, $e_1 = P_1 \Delta X_1 / X_1^* \Delta P_1$ so that:

$$\Delta P_1 = P_1 \Delta X_1 / X_1^* e_1 \tag{4}$$

Now substitute (4) in (3):

$$DWL_1 = \tfrac{1}{2}(P_1 \Delta X_1^2)/X_1^* e_1 \tag{5}$$

A similar expression can be calculated for DWL_2. Now insert into the optimality requirement (2) and we obtain:

$$\frac{Z_1}{Z_2} = \frac{P_1 \Delta X_1^2 X_2^* e_2}{P_2 \Delta X_2^2 X_1^* e_1} = \frac{e_2}{e_1} \tag{6}$$

This result, $Z_1/Z_2 = e_2/e_1$, the 'inverse elasticity formula', confirms the implication arrived at earlier, that the more inelastic the demand for the product, the greater should be the percentage deviation from marginal cost. The price of each product should be set so that 'its percentage deviation from marginal cost is inversely proportionate to the item's price elasticity of demand'.[54] This can be shown to hold true generally, and not just in the highly simplified geometric example.

This socially optimal pricing rule is unlikely to be followed by any regulatory agency, however. The informational requirements are too exacting, and precise cost and demand schedules for all products cannot be known to the authorities. Without such information attempts at imposing optimal pricing behaviour would be futile. Even if that data was available it is doubtful if any quasi-political pricing body would employ them in the optimal manner. High demand elasticity generally means ready availability of substitutes. Low demand elasticity, conversely, tends to mean that people who want a certain product have few alternatives available to them and/or regard the product as a 'necessity'. When this is the case they would be likely to raise considerable and vocal objections to a relatively high price for such a product. The monolithic political mechanism, unlike the more pluralistic commercial market, works in such a way that overt pressure-group objections of this kind tend to be deferred to, irrespective of their overall social merits.

An unregulated profit-maximising firm, on the other hand, would adopt a pricing scheme at least qualitatively similar to the socially optimal one. In the short run overhead costs will be regarded by the firm as sunk, and the firm will then set $MR = MC$ for all products. Given that $MR_i = P_i(1 + 1/e_i)$ for any product i, where P_i is the selling price including mark-up, and given that $z_i = (P_i - MC_i)/MC_i$, then with profit maximisation:

$$MR = MC$$

so that:

$$P\left(1 + \frac{1}{e}\right) = \frac{P - MC}{Z} = \frac{P - MR}{Z}$$

and:

$$P\left(\frac{1+e}{e}\right) = \frac{P - \dfrac{P(1+e)}{e}}{Z}$$

cancelling and multiplying through by e we have:

$$1 + e = \frac{-1}{Z}$$

Thus in a two-product, profit-maximising firm, prices are set so that for products 1 and 2:

$$\frac{1 + e_1}{1 + e_2} = \frac{Z_2}{Z_1} \tag{7}$$

which is not dissimilar to equation (6).

A commercial firm does not operate under the political constraints on economic good sense which a regulatory agency does. It can, therefore, pursue this type of pricing policy. It will not, of course, any more than a government body, have the requisite information to take such pricing decisions. The critical factor, however, is not the different levels of information available to each but rather their differing motivations. '(U)nder a wide range of circumstances individual firms behave as if they were seeking rationally to maximise their expected returns . . . (with) full knowledge of the data needed to succeed in this attempt; *as if*, that is, they knew the relevant cost and demand functions'.[55] Whether the firm has or has not that information is irrelevant. If it behaves as though it had, then the underlying theory of equation (7) and the resulting implications for social and economic welfare are just as meaningful and valuable as they would be if profit maximising behaviour were an accurate description of reality.

A regulatory agency, then, may take politically popular decisions on price which are economically and socially unsound. A profit-maximising firm, conversely, will take pricing decisions which are not dissimilar to the economic and social optimum but which, if subject to political scrutiny, may appear unacceptable and unjustifiable.

Douglas Cocks'[56] theory of pricing in a dynamically competitive situation comes to not dissimilar conclusions to Schankerman. In addition, where Schankerman possibly considers varying product qualities (as implied but not necessitated by his comparison of varying demand elasticities), Cocks explicitly embraces the possibility that competition takes place in dimensions other than price. Cocks' approach is that of comparative statics based on a modification of Clemens'[57] article on multiple-product pricing. He argues from the following premises:

(*a*) The development of new products is a primary objective of many firms. The preferred market position which such new products can provide is the main incentive for this objective.

(*b*) Firms will expand output to the point where the least profitable unit will be produced at a marginal cost equal to price. Unlike Clemens, Cocks does not lay stress on the use of idle capacity, but rather on the movement by firms towards meeting unfulfilled demand for drug therapy (by producing either major, minor or even insignificant advances over existing products).

(*c*) There is a high cross-elasticity of supply between therapeutic markets in both pharmaceutical production and R & D processes. This permits the demand curves under examination to be considered in

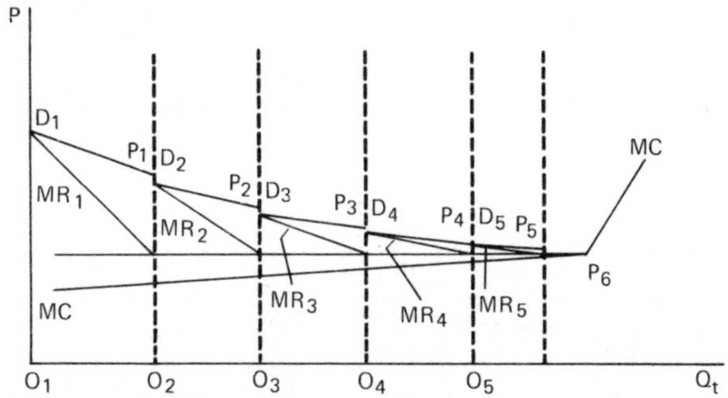

Fig. 4.5.
Source: Clemens, *op. cit.*

commensurate units (in terms of inputs required) to produce a heterogeneous range of outputs.

(*d*) There is low cross-elasticity of demand between a firm's products, *viz.* their demand curves tend to relate to different therapeutic areas.

(*e*) The market positions of the firm's various products range from strong market power (*e.g.* newly patented drugs) to perfect competition (*e.g.* multi-source, generic, commodity-like products).

Figure 4.5 is the basic, static situation, Clemens model. It shows five separate demand curves for one firm, with profits maximised where marginal revenue is equated in each and the limit set by the market with the perfectly elastic demand curve. Cocks then used Fig. 4.6 for a comparative statics analysis of drug-industry price and product competition. He asserts that 'price competition . . . would be reflected by a shift of the demand curves D_1 through D_5 downwards and towards greater elasticity'.

> (Figure 4.6) depicts the drug firm shown in (Fig. 4.5) in a subsequent period when it has successfully introduced a new drug significantly better than existing drug therapy. Demand curve D_6 represents this new drug. While the firm was developing this product, competitors could readily see the profit potential of the product associated with, say, D_5. They had an incentive to enter with products of their own, and such entry would cause the elasticity of D_5 to become greater. The introduction of the new product, D_6, alerts competitors to the profit potential of the new therapy also. At the same time the firm in (Fig. 4.6) is introducing its significant new product, it could also be entering product areas of competitive firms (D_7) with demand curves

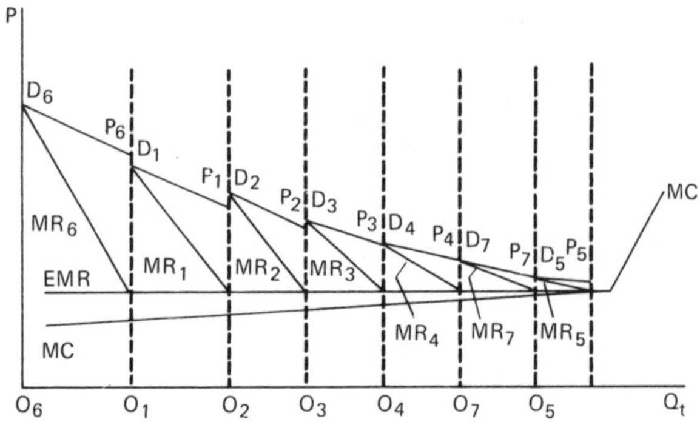

Fig. 4.6.
Source: Cocks, *op. cit.*

like D_5 in (Fig 4.5), or any other product area in which price is greater than ma.ginal cost. This increases the elasticity of the demand curves faced by these competitors.[58]

The equilibrium towards which this process moves would embody a price tending towards marginal cost for at least some firms in every therapeutic market where innovation took place. This is not unlike the tendency to Paretian optimality. If the P:MC ratio on the intra-marginal sales of all firms merely reflects differences in the R & D costs attributable to producing the relevant NCE for the intra-marginal markets the (hypothetical) outcome would be a very close approximation to perfectly competitive equilibrium. Moreover, even if the P:MC ratio does not do this, *i.e.* fall, allocative efficiency is still likely if these patients just on the margin of buying are provided with a drug offered by a firm operating at P = MC.[59]

The outcome of this argument is that the industry is not purely competitive in the sense of static microtheory. Rather, the pricing behaviour of the industry suggests a competitive process with a welfare loss in the static sense but where the 'monopoly rents' implied are actually the sources of funds for the R & D which develops new products in the future. Thus the dynamic element must be considered. These 'rents' represent social-opportunity costs in the sense that they partially represent what society forgoes if prices behave in the manner suggested and not in the manner predicted by the standard theory of perfect competition. Thus in order to obtain NCEs in the future, society must forgo certain benefits today represented by product prices being greater than marginal manufacturing costs. This 'welfare loss' is the social marginal cost of R & D so that if this is added to the 'production costs' the total marginal social cost may well come close to being equated with the product price. The pricing outcome in practice would imply that *for any individual existing drug* the R & D marginal social cost is transitory as prices are eroded over time so that for the industry as a whole, new products must be introduced on a continuum in order to maintain this marginal social cost in order, in turn, to provide R & D on a continuing basis.

In brief the static model of perfect competition is an inappropriate tool with which to analyse the economic performance of an innovative industry like pharmaceuticals. Even when the microeconomic model is extended to embrace oligopoly in a static framework it still fails to take account of the richness and complexity of the real-life variables that determine product price and quality. A theory is required that is both dynamic with respect to price and quality and defines marginal cost sufficiently accurately to embrace innovative expenditures. Only then can meaningful price: marginal cost comparisons be made.

5 Politics and Prices – Recent Evidence

In this chapter we examine some recent work on drug-industry pricing. Some writers have investigated whether or not drug prices tend to be stable or flexible. Others have examined the impact on price levels of patent expiry. Industry entry has also been examined as an influence on pricing behaviour. The relationship between monetary price and product quality in Reekie's work in the British industry is reported on. We then attempt to answer the question as to whether prescribers are price sensitive, other things being equal. Finally, the British study reported on is extended to the American market.

STUDIES IN AMERICA

The general argument is sometimes made that in oligopolistic industries prices are administered and do not respond to changes in demand and supply conditions. Sanjaya Lall has explicitly argued that drug-industry prices are inflexible. He writes '. . . that the pricing policies of the large drug firms are based on purely monopolistic principles . . . rather than on the socially responsible one of lowering them after recovering research costs'[1]

There is some limited evidence to support this charge. For example, Markham computed prices for individual products for the ten-year period 1949–59. Of the 308 individual drug product prices observed, more than 50 per cent did not change at all during the ten-year period.[2] But this and other previously published pricing studies were based on stated wholesale prices as reflected in published price lists. It is now generally recognized that price lists represent initial offering prices from which various discounts and deals are frequently made. One way to reflect such special pricing activity is to observe the resulting retail-transactions prices, as an indirect measure of variations in manufacturing prices.

Table 5.1. Price flexibility in the anti-infective product set

Product	No. possible price changes	No. changes of at least 1, 2, 4, 8 index points			
		1	2	4	8
1	9	7	4	2	0
2	9	6	3	0	0
3	9	8	8	7	4
4	9	6	5	3	1
5	9	7	6	3	0
6	9	7	2	1	0
7	9	5	4	3	2
8	9	6	5	0	0
9	9	8	6	6	3
10	9	5	4	1	1
11	9	9	7	4	2
12	8	8	7	3	1
Total	107	82	61	33	14

Source: Cocks and Virts, *op. cit.*, p. 360

The findings by Cocks and Virts[3] on drug prices in actual transactions are laid out in Table 5.1 for individual anti-infective products. In Table 5.2 price changes are averaged over the leading products in ten ethical drug product sets. These tables indicate that considerably more price flexibility is present in pharmaceuticals than would be revealed by a study of published price lists alone. Moreover price movements tend to have been downwards. In Table 5.3 Cocks and Virts show the price trends of leading products in three therapeutic product sets. The general trend of prices is downwards from 1962 to 1971. In the anti-infective product set, the price index of leading product declined by almost 32 per cent. It is notable also that the leading product at the beginning of the period generally experiences substantial price declines during the nine-year period. In many instances the price declines of products that were the leading products at the beginning of the period were greater than the other products.

In Table 5.4 the price indices of ten ethical drug product sets are summarised. From 1962 to 1967 prices in each of the ten product sets declined. With the onset of general inflation in the USA after 1966, some of the price increases resulted in levels above the 1962 base. But even this was true for only two of the ten product sets, by 5 and 8 per

Table 5.2. Average price changes of the leading products in ten ethical drug product sets

Product set	Average No. possible price changes	Average No. changes of at least 1,2,4,8 index points				No. different firms in product set in	
		1	2	4	8	1962	1971
1. Anti-infectives	8.9	6.8	5.1	2.8	1.2	7	8
2. Analgesic and anti-inflammatory	8.3	5.8	3.5	1.3	0.4	7	8
3. Psychopharmaceutical	8.6	6.2	4.6	1.9	0.2	7	7
4. Cough and cold	8.8	7.6	4.2	2.6	1.2	7	7
5. Antihypertensive diuretic	8.4	6.1	3.6	0.8	0.1	6	6
6. Vitamin and hematinic	8.7	6.7	4.8	2.6	0.6	9	8
7. Oral contraceptive	4.6	4.0	3.6	2.3	0.3	1	6
8. Anticholinergic and antispasmodic	9.0	6.8	4.4	1.9	0.4	8	8
9. Antiobesity	9.0	6.1	4.4	2.5	0.4	6	6
10. Diabetic therapy	8.3	4.8	3.2	1.7	0.3	4	4

Source: Cocks and Virts, *op. cit.*, p. 361

Table 5.3. Price trends for selected therapeutic classes (1962–71)

Product (Rank Order, 1962)	Anti-infective product set 1962	Anti-infective product set 1971	Analgesic and anti-inflammatory product set 1962	Analgesic and anti-inflammatory product set 1971	Psychopharmaceutical product set 1962	Psychopharmaceutical product set 1971
1.	100	70.3	100	88.4	100	84.4
2.	100	93.8	100	105.1	100	93.2
3.	100	33.1	100	104.5	100	106.1
4.	100	65.6	100	105.0	100	105.4
5.	100	72.6	100	109.0	100	104.2
6.	100	82.1	100	100.8	100	105.5
7.	100	67.8	100	89.6	100	113.2
8.	100	92.5	100	108.3	100	64.8
9.	100	47.7	100	106.5	...	94.0[4]
10.	100	80.3	100	103.3	...	89.1[5]
11.	100	40.5	...	88.9[2]	–	–
12.	...	79.9[1]	...	92.5[3]	–	–
Price index of leading products BLS	100	68.2	100	98.0	100	91.7
consumer price index for prescriptions	100	94.6	100	94.6	100	94.6

Notes:– [1] 1963 = 100
[2] 1965 = 100
[3] 1967 = 100
[4] 1963 = 100
[5] 1965 = 100
BLS = U.S. Bureau of Labour Statistics

Source: Cocks and Virts, *op. cit.*, pp. 355–8.

Table 5.4. Price indices of leading products in ten ethical drug product sets

	Product set	1962	1963	1964	1965	1966	1967	1968	1969	1970	1971
1.	Vitamin and hematinic	100	100.3	98.5	97.4	97.4	97.2	97.1	100.4	101.3	101.3
2.	Anti-infective	100	92.8	90.4	87.9	84.9	77.6	74.8	73.7	71.3	68.2
3.	Cough and cold	100	107.0	101.6	99.9	99.7	99.5	99.9	104.5	105.7	108.3
4.	Analgesic and anti-inflammatory	100	100.7	100.0	103.0	99.0	97.5	95.7	96.3	95.6	98.0
5.	Antihypertensive and diuretic	100	98.4	97.4	97.2	96.1	95.8	93.1	91.4	92.3	93.4
6.	Psychopharmaceutical	100	99.4	97.7	96.3	95.3	94.8	91.6	93.4	92.2	91.7
7.	Antiobesity	100	103.1	101.4	100.8	99.2	99.7	98.6	100.2	101.3	105.1
8.	Oral contraceptive	100	85.9	79.7	76.3	75.5	70.6	69.1	73.0	75.3	77.0
9.	Anticholinergic and antispasmodic	100	101.2	99.8	99.8	99.9	98.8	99.0	99.1	101.0	100.7
10.	Diabetic therapy	100	95.7	89.0	87.1	83.8	81.7	82.3	81.6	80.3	81.0
BLS consumer price index for prescriptions		100	97.6	96.3	95.2	95.1	93.4	91.8	93.0	94.5	94.6

Source: Cocks and Virts, *op. cit.*, p. 359.

Table 5.5. New entrants and their effective prices at time of entry compared to the price of polycillin (100 capsules 250 mg)

	1964	1966	1967	1968	1969	1972	1973
Polycillin (Bristol)	$26.85	27.09	25.88	21.67	21.54	15.75	13.80
Penbritin (Ayerst)	26.00						
Omnipen (Wyeth)		25.58					
Principen (Squibb)			19.20				
Amcill (Parke Davis)				21.12			
Alpen (Lederle)					19.21		
Totacillin (Beecham)					20.00		
Pensyn (Upjohn)						8.42	
SK–Ampicillin (SKF)							11.61
Pen-A(Pfizer)							6.35

Source: Schwartzman, *op. cit.*, p. 280.

cent respectively. For two other product sets, the price indices in 1971 were virtually at the same level as in 1962. For three product sets price decreases between 1962 and 1971 were substantial, approximating to a 20 per cent decline.

David Schwartzman carried out a study of price levels for products which are multi-source. When patents expire, products are no longer unique to their original innovator and a few licensed competitors who pay royalities to the patentee. Instead any manufacturer who cares to do so can enter the market and produce and sell chemical equivalents. The principal market in which patent protection for many large selling drugs has disappeared has been antibiotics. This market, according to Schwartzman 'became a jungle', with prices falling to levels which were well below those at the beginning of the 1960s.[4]

Even in the case of products where patent protection still existed and licensees entered the market, entrants generally adopted a lower price than existing firms. This competitive pressure tended to force down the prices of existing producers of the drug. In the case of ampicillin, for example, only one product (Amcill) failed to enter the market at a lower price than the leading product (Polycillin), and also lower than the products which had entered earlier (Table 5.5).

Schwartzman also discovered that although some firms 'with larger market shares tended to hold back (from retaliatory price cutting, *in each case* they) eventually were forced to cut their prices due to losses in their shares of the market'.[5]

Telser,[6] covered a similar time period to that of Schwartzman (1963–72) but examined virtually the entire industry and did not restrict himself to antibiotics nor to multi-source drugs. Entry, as defined by Telser, was the proportion of sales (in dollars) in 1972 in a therapeutic category by firms that were absent from the category in 1963 or some other initial specified date. Thus the measure was more closely related to successful or net entry than it was to a gross entry count of firms or products such as that displayed in Table 5.5.[7]

Telser's main argument is illustrated in Fig. 5.1 *DD* and (*D,No*) are the initial demand and supply curves of an industry with *N* firms. Thus if *N* is constant the minimum total cost of producing *Oq* is *OqAB*. R_1 is the equilibrium position with *Oqo* representing the optimal supply response of the *N* firms. If demand slips to D_1 D_1 the new equilibrium of demand and supply is R_2. But this is not the optimal supply response. Telser argues that this movement along the supply curve by the existing *N* firms would be less than optimal. A superior result would be obtained if *N* increased as a consequence of entry and the whole supply function

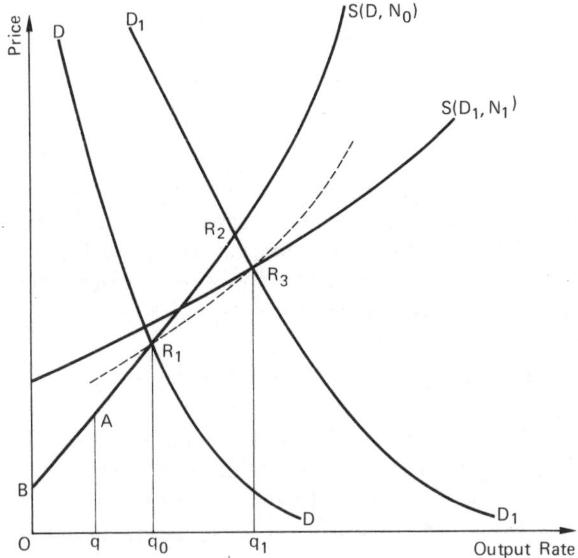

Fig. 5.1. Supply response to shifting demand
Source: Telser, *op. cit.*, p. 209.

shifted to $S(D_1, N_1)$. At R_3 it will be less costly to satisfy the increase in demand than at R_2.

Telser's main conclusion with respect to price was that prices tend to fall in response to entry (the R_2 to R_3 movement). Entry itself (the R_1 to R_2 movement) was an increasing function of sales growth, market size, and promotional intensity, and a decreasing function of N and of the stability of share of all existing firms' sales from one year to the next in any given market. There was a statistically significant and inverse relationship between the rate of change of prices and industry entry.

Entry appears to be important as a determinant of price in the USA, as illustrated by both Schwartzman and Telser. It is therefore worth recording the results of a British study by Reekie which showed that in 1966 more than one-third of the firms in the UK industry (26 firms out of 71) had entered since 1950[8] and accounted for over 30 per cent of the industry's sales by 1966. This analysis also showed that, except for the newest entrants which had not had time to establish themselves and grow, there was no indication that new entrants since 1950 were typically smaller firms than those established in earlier years. It appears that 'unlike more traditional industries, both rapid relative and absolute growth can occur soon after entry.'[9]

PRICE AND QUALITY IN THE UK

In a recent study of pricing behaviour in the UK industry[10] Reekie compared NCE price, quality and market success. All new chemical entities introduced on to the UK market between 1962 and 1970 were identified. The sample totalled 125 compounds which were sold in the 35 submarkets (out of a possible 80 or so) which accounted, in 1973, for 84.2 per cent of all NHS sales.

The sample of compounds was drawn from an original list compiled for NEDO's study of 'Innovative Activity in the Pharmaceutical Industry'.[11] The 125 entities were ranked on a '1' to '5' scale during the NEDO study by pharmacological or clinical experts in the relevant discipline. Table 5.6 provides the definitions of the five rankings for therapeutic value. The assessments were made in the light of the historical situation at the actual date of launch. Thus a fundamental advance at its time of introduction would be ranked '1' even if it was quickly superseded. 'Advantages' included reduction in side-effects as well as improved therapeutic response. The two main economic variables examined were price and market performance. In addition to these, information was assembled relating to whether or not a launch was rapidly succeeded by another new product introduction.

Price must clearly relate to treatment costs and not to volume of tablets, capsules or whatever. In this study, price was measured by daily dosage cost. Indices of relative price were constructed by dividing the price of the NCE by either an unweighted or weighted average of the prices of the leading three or five products in the relevant therapeutic sub-market in the year of introduction. Market success was measured

Table 5.6. Definitions for five rankings of 'therapeutic value'

1. Fundamental new medicine, of major clinical significance.
2. Important new medicine, offering substantial advantages for a majority of patients.
3. Useful new medicine, offering advantages for a minority of patients.
4. New medicine offering only marginal advantages over previously available therapies.
5. New medicine offering little or no advantage over previously available therapies.

Table 5.7. Frequency distributions of relative innovative prices (products analysed by therapeutic value)

Rank	Nos	>4.0–4.0	<4.0–2.0	<2.0–1.33	<1.33–1.0	<1.0
1	19	3	9	3	2	2
2	23	2	10	3	1	7
3	22	1	6	7	2	6
4	28	3	1	7	6	11
5	33	0	4	7	7	15
	125	9	30	27	18	41

Source: Reekie, *op. cit.*

by the share achieved in the relevant sub-market during either the first two calendar years of a product life or during the first three years.

Table 5.7 provides frequency distributions for the first of the four indices of relative price analysed by therapeutic rank.[12] Approximately one-third of all innovations was introduced at lower prices than the leading available substitutes. (The ratio of innovation price to existing products' prices was less than unity.) From this level a continuum of pricing ratios was observed through to levels where the innovations were introduced at prices which were a multiple of four or more times as great as that of existing market leaders. Finally, inspection of the data indicated that the majority of the observations tend to lie either to the top and left of the tables or to the bottom and right. In other words, high therapeutic value innovations tend to be priced more highly than do those with minimal or zero advantages over existing therapies.

Table 5.8. Frequency distribution of market performance (products analysed by therapeutic values)

Rank	Nos	0–5%	5–10%	10–20%	20%
1	19	6	1	4	8
2	23	9	2	3	9
3	22	4	5	4	9
4	28	15	9	2	2
5	33	23	5	5	0
	125	57	22	18	28

Source: Reekie, *op. cit.*

With respect to market performance Table 5.8 shows that most minor innovations obtained a market share of 5 per cent or less after two years (or 7.5 per cent or less after three years). The innovations of major rank achieved market shares of over 20 per cent in two years (or over 30 per cent in three years).

Regression analysis indicated that price was significantly and positively associated with therapeutic ranking. But price was inversely and significantly associated with the entry of a competing NCE within two years of the launch of the innovation under study. In other words, holding product quality constant, firms will adopt a low price for a NCE if competitive entry is a real threat in the immediate future. Such behaviour is perfectly credible in the pharmaceutical industry where firms know each other's R & D plans well in advance. (Clearly this is not the case with long-term R & D project selection plans, which will generally be highly confidential.) This advance knowledge will partly be due to scientific gossip, but more importantly will be due to the need to carry out the various formal tests for purposes of registration with the Medicines Commission. Clinical trials, in particular, are difficult to conceal from competitors.

New pharmaceuticals, then, can be introduced at a high price designed to extract the highest possible revenue when demand (for these products) is relatively inelastic, and thereafter gradually reduced in price through the product life-cycle. A rationale for this policy, what Joel Dean[13] called 'skimming pricing', is easy to give. A high initial cash flow is required to repay as rapidly as possible the innovative outlays of the firm; secondly, as time passes price sensitivity is increasing as the government exerts pressure through the VPRS on the one hand, and competitors retaliate with similarly priced, but equally or possibly more advanced innovations of their own; finally lower-priced rivals will begin to appear as patent expiry approaches.

The alternative extreme is a policy of 'penetration pricing'. This occurs where prices are set at a relatively low level on market launch. It may be adopted when the product represents only a minor departure from those previously available and is unable to command a substantial premium over existing not dissimilar, alternatives. It may also be used as a discouraging 'keep-out' policy in anticipation of new and rival entrants.

Between these extremes there will be a continuum of possible relative price levels. It is easy to show how price discrimination over time (skimming) can be perfectly justifiable in welfare terms. Price discrimination is *not* a perjorative term. It indicates merely that a product is being sold at different (non-marginal cost related) prices. Skimming pricing is a form of price discrimination[14] in that the same product is being sold at different points in time at different prices. It can be justified on welfare grounds in that it enables a firm to appropriate to itself 'consumers' surplus' and so increase producer's profits. This is economically desirable where marginal costs are very low (as in pharmaceuticals) or are zero. In such a situation the profit available to a firm which did not discriminate by 'skimming' could be inadequate to pay for the innovative investment required for a new pharmaceutical product. Consider Fig. 5.2, *DE* represents the demand curve for a pharmaceutical product with a four-year life span. We will assume zero marginal cost. The profit maximising price and output level for the firm is £0.5 and 2*Q* units spread over four years. At this point MR=MC (since with a linear demand curve MR always bisects a horizontal line drawn from the £ axis to the demand curve at its mid-point). With a zero discount rate the firm would have sales revenue equal to *ABCO*; provided this exceeds the costs of innovative investment (R & D and the like) the firm would develop the product and sell it as described. Consumers would additionally receive, 'free' as it were, welfare benefits equal to the consumers surplus triangle *ABD*.

There are two welfare defects in this situation, however. First, if the innovative investment costs exceed *ABCO* (*i.e.* £1 million) the drug

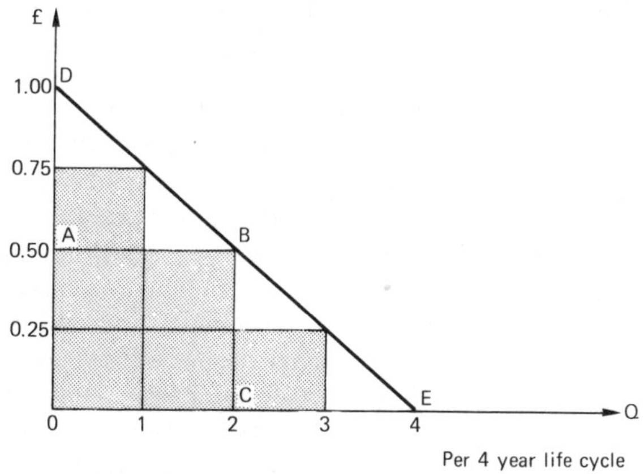

Fig. 5.2. Hypothetical demand curve for a drug with a four-year life span.

would not be developed, despite the fact that at output level *C* total (consumers' surplus plus producer's revenue) welfare equals *ODBC* (£1.5 million). Second, total possible gross consumer welfare is not restricted to *ODBC* but is equal to the whole area under the demand curve, *ODE* (£2 million). A simple, non-skimming, profit maximising price of £0.5 results in a 'deadweight-loss' of *BCE*. No firm will produce 4*Q* units in four years under such circumstances. The firm *would* produce 4*Q* units and *would* invest up to £2 million in R & D, however, if it could practice price discrimination of the skimming variety. This is because, say, given equal annual outputs of 1*Q* unit, it sold at £0.75 in year 1, £0.50 in year 2, £0.25 in year 3 and a price approaching zero in year 4, then it would earn a revenue equal to the shaded area of the diagram. This is an area exceeding *OABC* and tending to approach *ODE*, or £2 million.

This analysis is a minor variant of the well-known arguments put forward by Dupuit,[15] the father of modern welfare economics, when he attempted to justify the construction of a bridge which a *non*-price discriminating, toll charging monopolist would consider to be a bad investment. The ability to price-discriminate depends, of course, on the presence of a degree of innovative monopoly protected by patent or other legal arrangements.

Studies in the USA have shown that drug prices are not as inflexible as is sometimes claimed. Entry is apparently one potent factor exerting downward pressure in prices. This is at odds with the thesis of those investigators who assert that there is no price competition in the industry, that prices are 'administered' and that doctors are price-insensitive.

In the UK industry entry has also been a prominent characteristic. Price-levels for NCEs are associated with the degree of therapeutic novelty they have in relation to existing products. Prices are thus determined in large part by the level of competition perceived to exist in the market place. This depends in turn on the extent to which the innovation will provide a product (or characteristics) monopoly over existing product offerings. It is also dependent on whether such a monopoly is expected to be brief or prolonged, and whether further entry by a superseding NCE is anticipated or not. It appears, therefore that there is price competition in the drug industry. What has not yet been demonstrated is whether or not prescribers are sensitive to price differentials. However, the evidence strongly supports the view that pharmaceutical firms behave as though prescribers are, in fact, significantly price-conscious.

PRICE AND QUALITY IN THE USA

The results and inferences obtained in Reekie's UK study may not be transferable to the American situation. In the UK it could be argued that there is a strong monopsony buyer, the NHS, exerting countervailing power on the industry which has resulted in effectively competitive behaviour. Certainly this monopsony power appears to have brought about a lower overall price level in the UK than in many other countries.[16] Casual theorising, however, might lead one to reject the view that the monopsony cudgel, at least as epitomised by the VPRS, produced the detailed, rational and competitive pricing behaviour which apparently exists. This for two main reasons. First, the study covered the prices of innovations in their first two or three years of life, from 1962 to 1970. The version of the VPRS which operated for every year of this time-span provided for either a two-or a four-year 'freedom period' during which firms could pitch prices at levels which they themselves considered appropriate. In short, the VPRS did not apply to innovations during most of the study period. Secondly, the 125 innovations were each compared with three or five existing products. That is, up to 750 different product prices were covered by this investigation. It seems improbable that the (unavoidably) limited-scale product-by-product negotiating style of the VPRS of the 1960s would produce the finely detailed results obtained here for such a large number of products.

One would, however, anticipate similar results in countries without a national health service; for example, the USA. There, doctors have long been aware that different patients have different incomes and so vary in ability to pay. This is reflected by their use of price discrimination[17] and their levying of varying fees for the same treatment. It seems unlikely that such doctors will be price-sensitive agents on behalf of their patients' needs for some parts of the total health care 'package' they provide but not for others (namely, drugs). If we bear in mind that the doctor will be assessing the cost effectiveness of a drug, given the patient's total sociomedical needs, it does seem probable that on occasion — if not many occasions — he will deliberately prescribe cheaper and/or older and/or less effective or less potent and/or generic, unbranded products. Also, there is the additional price constraint in the USA that the patient can shop around for the cheapest retail pharmacy to fill his prescription (resale price maintenance is illegal in many States). Patient price-awareness of this sort, will, *a priori*, also influence prescriber price-consciousness. When the disease

Table 5.9. New chemical entities analysed by price and Food and Drug Administration rating (1958–75) (All data refer to date of product launch.)

		FDA rating criteria			
		Important therapeutic gain	Modest therapeutic gain	Little or no therapeutic gain	Total
	Low	7	12	53	72
Price	Medium	6	13	44	63
	High	16	9	11	36
	Total	29	34	108	171

Notes: 'Low price' = price ratios of unity and below
'Medium price' = price ratios of over 1.0 and of 1.5 and below
'High price' = price ratios over 1.5

Price = P_{NCE}/P_c

where P_{NCE} = dollar sales of the NCE made through new prescriptions divided by number of new prescriptions written for the NCE, *i.e.* the average price of a new prescription for the NCE.

P_c = the weighted average price of a new prescription for the relevant leading competitive drugs; given the oligopolistic nature of the markets the number of competitors examined was either three, four or five and these products accounted for the bulk of all the remaining turnover in the market not attributable to the NCE; the weights awarded being the relative sales figures of the competing products.

Important therapeutic gain: Drug may provide effective therapy or diagnosis (by virtue of greatly increased efficacy or safety) for a disease not adequately treated or diagnosed by any marketed drug, or provide markedly improved treatment of a disease through improved efficacy or safety (including decreased abuse potential).

Modest therapeutic gain: Drug has a modest, but real advantage over other available marketed drugs; *e.g.* somewhat greater effectiveness, decreased adverse reactions, less frequent dosing in situations where frequent dosage is a problem etc.

Little or no therapeutic gain: Essentially duplicates in medical importance and therapy for one or more already existing drugs.

Source: Reekie, W. Duncan, 'Price and Quality Competition in the United States Drug Industry', *Journal of Industrial Economics* (1978).

is one which requires continuous, repeat prescription therapy (*e.g.* rheumatism) as opposed to a single short-period regimen (*e.g.* infections) this effect, a *fortiori*, will be enhanced.

The natural follow-up study to the British investigation was to replicate it for the American market. This replication, with modifications in methodology and scope is reported on in the following pages.

Table 5.9 categorises all NCEs which were introduced onto the US drug market between 1958 and 1975 by price relative to competing products and by Food and Drug Administration (FDA) rating criteria.[18] Over 40 per cent of the 171 NCEs were introduced at lower prices than leading available substitutes. (72 NCEs, 42.19 per cent, fell into the 'low' price category.) Approximately 20 per cent of all innovations were introduced at 'high' prices which could achieve multiples well in excess of the over 1.5 ratio used in the table. Finally, inspection of the data indicates that innovations providing 'important therapeutic gains' tend to be priced more highly than do NCEs with 'modest or no' therapeutic advantages over existing products.[19] This is illustrated by the fact that the majority of the observations lie diagonally across the table from bottom left to top right.

The findings fit well within the behaviour predicted by simple price theory. If markets are composed of rival or 'effectively competitive' suppliers, if price collusion is weak or non-existent, and if product demand is not wholly inelastic, then firms *will* price major breakthroughs above the price of previously available alternatives. They will be able to do so because consumers will be willing to pay more for the more productive new products. The demand curve for the new product will be above and to the right of existing demand curves by an amount approximating the value placed by the market on the differential. Minor variants, however, would have to be priced below competitors so as to give them the price advantage necessary with which to make a successful market entry. The demand curve for these new products would be that portion of the relevant market demand curve to the right of the ruling market price. 'Marketable' medicines and 'therapeutically new' drugs, then, do not seem to be mutually exclusive.[20] High-priced drugs tend to provide the market with a high degree of therapeutic novelty. Minor advances or effective duplicates tend to provide the market with an alternative source of supply and/or with a real price reduction.

These results suggest considerable price flexibility was present over time. They are compatible with those of Cocks and Virts[21]

Schwartzman,[22] Telser[23] and Peltzman,[24] but directly contrary to the views of Lall.[25]

High initial prices do tend to be lowered. Conversely low prices seem to be met with competing price-cuts as existing firms strive to maintain market position in the face of entry. None of this is inexplicable in terms of simple competitive price theory. On the contrary, it is difficult to see how it can be regarded as typical of 'purely monopolistic principles' where firms ignore their 'social responsibility' of lowering prices 'after recovering research costs.[26] It is undoubtedly true that the interpretation that the data lend themselves to has no place for altruistic social responsibility. But the economist's task is to examine the market process with a view to ascertaining how a socially satisfactory economic performance can be attained. When he is satisfied that there are no barriers to the market achieving this goal (such as 'monopolistic principles' and practices) and if this goal is being achieved, then his task is complete. The evidence is presented in Table 5.10.

Table 5.10. Price statistics relating to all new chemical entities launched in the United States drug market (1958–75)

	Year 1	Year 2	Year 3	Year 4
Mean	1.618	1.519	1.345	1.287
Mode	1.073	0.998	1.061	1.35
Median	1.104	1.119	1.073	1.084
Maximum	15.516	11.969	5.128	5.449
Minimum	0.251	0.368	0.371	0.402
Range	15.265	11.601	4.757	5.047
n	185	175	163	146
Variance	3.577	2.022	0.709	0.500
F ratio	1.769 (Years 1–2)	2.852 (Years 2–3)	1.418 (Years 3–4)	
	(all significant at the 1% level in Snedecor's Table for the Variance Ratio)			
Coefficient of variation	1.169	0.936	0.626	0.549

Notes: Year 1 is generally the first full calendar year of a NCE's life cycle. This could be any year from 1958 to 1975.

Years 2, 3 and 4 are the relevant years succeeding year of launch. The data series ended in 1975. All NCE's are included in this analysis irrespective of whether or not the FDA had at the time of study rated them.

Source: Reekie, *op. cit.*

As would be expected from Table 5.9 there is a wide dispersion of prices shown in year 1 in Table 5.10. (A range and a variance of 15.265 and 3.577 respectively.) Such a wide dispersion in the asking price according to Stigler 'is a manifestation — and, indeed, it is the measure — of ignorance in the market'.[27] Stigler qualified this assertion in an important way for the purpose of this study. 'Dispersion is a biased measure of ignorance because there is never absolute homogeneity in the commodity . . . But it would be metaphysical and fruitless to assert that all dispersion is due to heterogeneity.'

In other words, one would expect some price dispersion to persist over time because of continuing drug quality differences. On the other hand, to the extent that it exists due to *ex ante* entrepreneurial activity one would expect it to narrow over time if the competitive process is at work. If it did not so narrow than changes, *ex post*, of monopoly behaviour would have some justification. The price data do remain significantly associated with the therapeutic rating scale over each of the four observed years. They also show (in Table 5.10) that the variance drops significantly between each pair of years.[28] High initial prices tend to fall, and low prices to rise. Diagrammatically, the dispersion of prices moves from a distribution akin to $D = 1$ to $D = 2$ in Fig. 5.3. The mean shifts from 1.618 to 1.287, depicted as $M = 1$ and $M = 2$ respectively. Neither the median nor the modal prices move meaningfully.

As Stigler's discussion suggests, the prices are 'skewed to the right . . . because the seller of reproducible goods will have some minimum but no maximum limit on the price he can accept'.[29] The reduction of spread

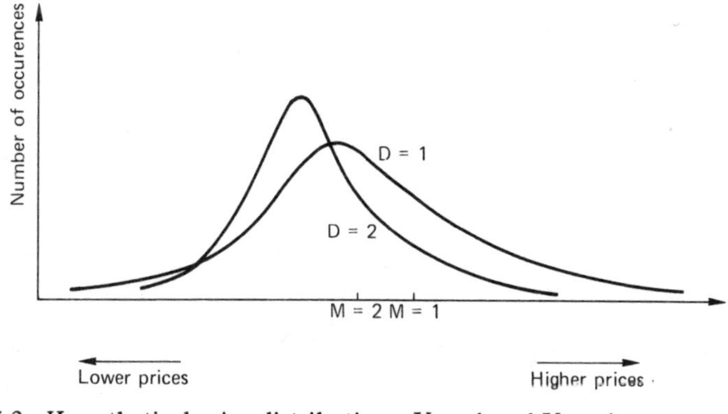

Fig. 5.3. Hypothetical price distributions. Year 1 and Year 4.

is consequently due more to the decrease of high than to the raising of low prices. This is also evident from the large falls of the relevant maxima *vis à vis* the small rises in the minima towards the averages in Table 5.2. Such large reductions in the extremely high values highlights a danger in our use of the variance ratio. The average (mean) real price of NCEs in year 4 is lower than in year 1. $M=2$ is lower and to the left of $M = 1$. Falls in the mean could be due mainly to reductions in magnitude of a few non-typical values. Moreover, the median averages, which would not be so affected, fall only slightly over the observation period. As a surety against being misled by comparisions of absolute measures of dispersion when a shifting mean is present, the Pearson coefficients of variations were calculated. These explicitly took account of the positions of the mean and fell by over 50 per cent between years 1 and 4. The spread of prices of NCEs over time thus narrows significantly in both relative and absolute terms.

Movement from $D=1$ to $D=2$ can result from four possible (non-mutually exclusive) alternatives. Since relative price:

$$P = \frac{P_{\text{NCE}}}{P_c}$$

where P_{NCE} is money price of the NCE and P_c is money price of competitors, then where P is relatively low it will tend upwards towards the average, either as a consequence of (i) P_{NCE} rising relatively more rapidly than P_c; or (ii) P_c falling relatively more rapidly than P_{NCE}; and where P is relatively high it will tend downwards towards the average either as a consequence of (iii) P_{NCE} falling relatively more rapidly than P_c; or (iv) P_c rising relatively more rapidly than P_{NCE}.

In each of these four alternative cases the second component in the expression may, of course, be static or moving in the opposite direction from the first.

Alternatives (ii) and (iii) imply the competitive responses one would expect from existing firms operating on a profit maximising basis as they gain and assimilate information on changing cost and demand conditions. These fit within a model of workable competition in an industry. Alternative (i) would represent the action of a firm with some degree of innovative monopoly power but which had initially misjudged the extent to which the NCE would give it an opportunity for pricing at relatively high levels. It is difficult to think of a plausible explanation for (iv) other than non-rational, non-profit maximising behaviour.[30]

Neither of explanations (i) and (iv) are likely reasons for the narrowing of dispersion.Moreover, both fail to fit the empirical facts. For example, Table 5.3 shows the wholesale and consumer price indices for drugs and also the average prescription price for 1958–75 (the period under examination). The indices have tended to fall or remain steady for all but the last year or so of the series. Average prescription prices, conversely, provide an indication of the simple arithmetic mean prescription price paid by consumers to pharmacists. In contrast to both the WPI and the CPI this has been rising steadily over the period of study. The solution to this apparent paradox lies in well-known index number problems. 'Average prescription price' shows prices actually paid by consumers, irrespective of size or composition of prescription. While 'the CPI index is so designed that it does not reflect the impact of new and costly products which may be introduced on the market and replace older and less expensive drugs'.[31]

In terms of our analysis average P_c (*i.e.* a base-weighted index) is falling over time while average P_{NCE} is sufficiently highly above P_c at launch to raise the average prescription price. This, of course, implies that the large numbers of NCEs priced below P_c (Table 5.9) do not generally achieve a high volume of sales relative to costlier NCEs. If they did then the discrepancy between the drug price indices and the average prescription price series would be much less or even reversed. None of this general evidence provides support for the explanations designated (i) or (iv). If competitive price-cutting behaviour (ii) and (iii) does in fact, account for the tightening of price spread noted in Table 5.10 the Table 5.11 does nothing to disprove such hypotheses. Rather, a comparison of columns (*a*) and (*d*) tends to suggest that NCEs priced at high initial levels not only experience relative but also monetary price declines, and that those priced towards the penetration end of the high:low launch price continuum prompt monetary price cuts in competing products.

An attempt was made to measure the elasticity of demand for NCEs by estimating a log linear function of the form

$$Q_{it} = aP_{it}^{b}N_{it}^{c}u^{e} \qquad (1)$$

where i and t denote a particular NCE and year respectively, Q is the ratio of the number of new prescriptions written in the relevant therapeutic market to total new prescriptions in that market and P is the ratio P_{NCE}/P_c. N is one plus the cumulative number of competing

Table 5.11. Ethical pharmaceutical preparations, wholesale price index: prescriptions; consumer price index; and average prescription price (1958–75)

1967 = 100

	(a) Drugs: WPI	(b) Drugs: CPI	(c) Price: $	(d) Index
1958	n.a.	113.1	3.08	84.8
1959	n.a.	115.7	3.14	85.5
1960	n.a.	115.3	3.22	88.7
1961	108.2	111.5	3.27	90.8
1962	105.6	107.1	3.26	89.8
1963	104.0	104.5	3.35	92.3
1964	103.9	103.1	3.42	94.2
1965	103.2	102.0	3.48	95.9
1966	102.6	101.8	3.56	98.1
1967	100.0	100.0	3.63	100.0
1968	99.0	98.3	3.70	101.9
1969	99.5	99.6	3.86	106.3
1970	99.3	101.2	4.02	110.7
1971	99.0	101.3	4.19	115.4
1972	99.1	100.9	4.32	119.0
1973	99.9	100.5	4.45	122.6
1974	104.2	102.9	4.70	129.5
1975	113.2	109.3	5.20	143.2

Sources: (*a*) and (*b*) U.S. Bureau of Labour Statistics; (*c*) and (*d*) *American Druggist*, and John M. Firestone *op. cit.*

Note: The actual wholesale prices measured by transaction prices probably fell more than the list prices used by the BLS (*see* George J. Stigler and James Kindahl, *The Behaviour of Industrial Prices*, National Bureau of Economic Research (1970)). In particular they constructed an index of tranquiliser transaction prices which declined substantially during a period in which the corresponding BLS tranquiliser price index remained unchanged.

NCEs introduced in the relevant market. The equation may be written

$$\log Q_{it} = \log a + b \log P_{it} + c \log N_{it} + e \qquad (2)$$

Equation (2) was calculated across 25 sub-markets and over the period from 1958–75 for each of years 1 to 4 of a NCE's life. This quasi-combination of time series and cross-sectional analyses, coupled with the nature of the variables, can be justified on the grounds that identification is facilitated and that many other problems involved in demand estimation are also overcome.

Over time demand changes may be dramatic. For example, Firestone[32,33] argues that 'the factor that (has) had the greatest influence on the unit price of prescribed drugs has been the size of the prescription'. He, in fact, gives this as the main explanation for the disparity between columns (*b*) and (*d*) of Table 5.11. The dollar price figure for 1975, adjusted by Firestone for prescription size, is $3.33, a mere 11 cents rise over the 1960 figure. With Q defined in ratio form, however, we can assume that any systematic factors affecting drug demand, such as prescription size (or incomes) are accounted for in the equation. Second, in simple time series, index linking of prices and incomes data for purposes of comparisons of relative changes is not easy. Our definition of P (effectively an index-deflated price) and the use of a ratio for Q helps to overcome this problem. Equation (2) can consequently be regarded as a real income demand function and the value of b a Slutsky and not a Cournot elasticity measure. Third, time series alone is not wholly appropriate, given that we wish to contrast elasticities at different stages in the product life-cycle.

The comparative cross-sectional analysis reported on below helps to accomplish this latter objective. Nevertheless, cross-sectional studies are not necessarily problem-free. In particular propensities to purchase may vary market by market, and cross-elasticities of demand between markets may not be zero. Differing propensities to purchase are arguably not significant in this study. Unlike a contrast of differing regional or demographic markets where consumers may vary in tastes and preferences here the 'consumers' are always the same group of individuals in each market : all prescribing doctors in the USA. To the extent that the prices of complements vary, then the definition of Q in ratio form ensures that the impact of negative cross-elasticities is embodied in the equation. The definitions of the sub-markets were given by the data source and can be regarded as separating off groups of substitutes one from the other so partially eliminating the problem of positive cross-elasticities. Moreover our analysis extends over only the first four years of a NCE's life. This minimises the number of occasions on which a NCE is faced with direct competition from another NCE. When such a contingency does occur it is accounted for by the simple expedient of including variable N. The impact of such competition is least in year 1 and greatest in year 4 as succeeding launches of NCEs in the same therapeutic market become progressively more probable. Thus we assume, that sellers set P in each period and offer to sell indefinitely large amounts at that price during the period. Variation in *P* is therefore determined largely by non-demand-related factors and so demand is duly identified. The results are summarised in Table 5.12. They are not unambiguous. Nevertheless price elasticity appears to be lowest early in the life cycle, a finding perfectly consistent with industry entry theory. Price sensitivity is relatively less when incremental product quality is 'important' and greater when the therapeutic gain is 'modest'. This does not confirm the view that doctors are not very price-conscious.Pharmaceutical firms and drug prescribers are, in fact, acting in the way predicted by several of the theories of innovative pricing behaviour we have examined. The above results are consistent with the Cocks:Clemens model (Fig. 4.5 and 4.6), the Schankerman model (Fig. 4.4), and skimming pricing (Fig. 5.2). The various empirical studies reported on are inconsistent not with each other, but with the

Table 5.12. Demand elasticities analysed by FDA rating and product maturity

	FDA rating	
	Important therapeutic gain	Modest therapeutic gain
Year 1	1.03	1.11
Year 2	1.65	2.68
Year 3	1.30	1.79
Year 4	n.s.	2.83

Source: Reekie, 1978, *op. cit.*
Notes: n.s. = not statistically significant.
The negative elasticity signs have been discarded.
Figures are rounded to two decimal places.
No meaningful elasticity measures were obtained for products of 'little or no' therapeutic gain.

The poor showing of the model for NCEs of 'little or no' incremental gain can be explained by the fact that even a low price cannot obtain market success for a weak product. By year 4 (their most successful year) only 28 of the 98 NCEs in this category had achieved market shares of 5 per cent or more, only 15 of those achieved 10 per cent or more and only five of these 20 per cent or more. Only one of the 28 had a 'high' *P* ratio, and it had obtained a market share of under 10 per cent, this after the lapse of four years. 'Spurious product differentiation' would not appear to be a sensible policy for drug firms to pursue.

view that the industry is non-price competitive and suffers from 'administered pricing'.

THE MEANING OF PRICE COMPETITION

In the USA drug price regulation is considerably less overt than in Britain. Traditionally, health care has been financed directly by the consumer (unlike the NHS system which is 'free' at the point of consumption). Although government and private insurance schemes have been of growing importance, thus separating the patient from payment at time of treatment, the vast bulk of expenditure on drugs (as opposed to other items of treatment such as doctors' fees) is still paid directly by patients to some form of drug retailers (84.4 per cent by value of all prescriptions in 1976).[34]

The monopoly and insurance elements which are jointly present in the British market are effectively absent in the USA. But since similar competitive pricing patterns have been discovered in both the UK and the USA the British results cannot then be attributed to the effectiveness of the NHS (*via* the VPRS) as a monopsony buyer. The similar pricing patterns must be attributed rather to some common factor in both markets. On the demand side the common factor is probably the price sensitivity of prescribing doctors. On the supply side the common factor is the competitive behaviour of the firms who make up the industry. If is a valid inference then the exercise of monopsony regulation in the UK is essentially unnecessary, and secondly, the view that the industry is not price-competitive must be less soundly based than has been imagined in the past.

None of our discussions nor the work reported on in the preceding pages provides definitive conclusions. Nonetheless, collectively, the various theories and empirical investigations provide considerable insights into how pharmaceutical prices should be defined, how marginal costs should be viewed, how and when doctors are price-sensitive and, in consequence, in what direction regulatory activity should be channelled with a view to improving the industry's economic performance.

Price is not cash price. The real price of a pharmaceutical must be modified by the quality of the product. Like any other good or service, a pharmaceutical's selling price is measured by the amount of other goods and services the consumer must forgo in order to purchase the characteristics of the drug. For example, if an existing drug requires four pills per day to be consumed for one week at 10p per pill, with the additional requirement of confinement to bed, then the real price of that drug to the consumer is £2.80 (7 × 4 × 10p) *plus* the week's wages he has forgone by being confined to bed. (Alternatively if the total cost is borne by society through socialised medicine and health insurance, the social cost is the same, namely £2.80 plus the value of goods and services the patient could have produced had he been at work.) On the other hand, if an alternative drug becomes available at £2.00 per pill, to be consumed at a rate of one pill per day for three days with only three-day home confinement, then the real cost to the consumer is £6 plus only the proportion of one week's wages represented by three day's loss of work.

The new drug costs £6 for a full treatment, the first £2.80. But the second drug is by far the more competitive in terms of real price. The second drug's real price is £6 plus two days wages (for a five-day week), say £46; the first drug's price is £102.80 (for five-day week for a patient normally earning £20 per day). The second drug has lowered the price of treatment by £56.80. That is price competition in the real meaning of the phrase.

In the simple example just described, the new drug lowered the real price of treatment. If competition works we would expect the price of the existing drug to fall to combat the price advantage of the innovation. Since the quality of the existing product cannot be changed the alternation must occur in its cash price. The evidence presented above from a variety of studies on both sides of the Atlantic suggests that this is precisely what happens. As NCEs are introduced onto the market the cash prices of existing products are pushed down by competitive forces, and the elasiticity of demand for existing products increases. Doctors tend to continue prescribing older products only if they are reduced in cash price and their real price disadvantage relative to better quality products is minimised.

Similarly we have seen from the evidence that new drugs which do not reduce the real price of treatment *via* improved therapeutic quality, must, in order to enter the market, reduce the real price of treatment via a lower cash price. There is little or no evidence on the demand side of the drug market to suggest that doctors are unaware of real price differentials. Little support has been found for the view that drug prices need to be regulated by government because demand is highly inelastic.

Market entry, by innovations from existing drug firms, or by innovations from firms new to the industry, has played a major part in reducing real and monetary drug prices over the years. Thus on the supply side of the drug market there is again little to suggest that prices are at levels relative to marginal cost, which indicates the possession of monopoly power by drug firms, and so the need for price regulation by government. If entry (of either kind) is deemed to be declining, however, this situation may change. The first task of an anti-trust agency then, however, should not be to control prices but to ensure that entry barriers have not been raised either by existing firms to the industry or by governmental controls favouring existing firms at the expense of potential new entrants. In the next chapters we shall illustrate that, in recent years, entry by innovation has become a much less serious threat to existing firms.

6 Politics and Promotion

The Sainsbury Report alleged that drug-industry promotion was 'wasteful' in absolute terms. The reliability of the promotion in purveying information was also questioned. Doctors 'viewed representatives with scepticism, if not suspicion'.[1] It is not surprising, then, that against this background, the government is attempting to curb promotional expenditures and also to provide doctors with product information in its own right.

THE NATURE OF PROMOTION

Promotion expenditures accounted for around 14 per cent of the value of NHS sales in the years of the Sainsbury investigation.[2] By inference the figure was approximately the same in 1976. In July 1977, the Secretary of State for Social Services, David Ennals, announced that the government proposed to implement a reduction in promotional expenditure in two stages to an average of 12 per cent of NHS sales in 1977 and then to 10 per cent by 1979. This is to be done, not by banning expenditure outright but by disallowing ammounts over these figures for calculations of profitability and price in PPRS negotiations.

Is drug-industry promotion unreliable and misleading? One consistent feature of independent studies of doctors' attitudes over the years has been their indication of the usefulness and reliability of information provided by industry representatives (in sharp contrast to the Sainsbury findings). A Gallup Poll survey of GPs discovered that only 11 per cent of the sample view visits by representatives as a 'waste of time'. In fact 76 per cent of the sample found some or all of them to 'useful'. A 1975 study by Medical Surveys Ltd. found that 81 per cent of GPs were opposed to any externally imposed reduction in firms' expenditures on representatives.[3]

Two other more intensive studies have been conducted. One was the Sainsbury Survey, the other an investigation sponsored in 1975 by the Office of Health Economics (OHE) and conducted by Market Investigations Ltd.[3] Tables 6.1 and 6.2, both taken from the Sainsbury

Table 6.1. The proportion of general practitioners considering each source to be either very good or fairly good with respect to getting to know of the efficacy and the existence of new products

Main sources of information (in order of proportion rated either very good or fairly good for getting to know about EFFICACY of new products)	Proportion of general practitioners rating source as either very good or fairly good for getting to know about the EXISTENCE of new products	Proportion of general practitioners rating source as either very good or fairly good for getting to know about the EFFICACY of new products
	Per cent	Per cent
Articles in medical journals	76	83
Recommendations from consultants	71	79
Professional contacts with other doctors	59	68
Refresher courses	61	65
Drug firm representatives	78	61
Local clinical meetings	51	57
MIMS	67	50
Medindex	47	42
Drug firm meetings	37	33
Drug firm literature	52	23
Advertisements in medical journals	53	19

Source: Sainsbury, *op. cit.*, p. 131.

Table 6.2. The proportion of general practitioners selecting each source as the best one for finding out about new products

Source of information	Source considered best for finding out about the EXISTENCE of new products	Source considered best for finding out about the EFFICACY of new products
	Per cent	Per cent
Advertisement in journals	7	1
Articles in journals	19	31
Drug firm literature	10	2
Drug firm representatives	34	12
MIMS	7	3
Medindex	1	1
Recommendations from consultants	14	1
Professional contacts with other doctors	3	13
Local clinical meetings	2	4
Drug firm meetings	—	1
Refresher courses	3	7
	100	100

Source: Sainsbury, *op. cit.*, p. 132.

Table 6.3. Source of information which most influenced the general practitioner to prescribe the products

Source	Ultralanum (ointment)	Mogadon (sleeping pill)	Indocid (anti-inflammatory)	Lasix (diuretics)
	Per cent	Per cent	Per cent	Per cent
Advertisements in journals	1	–	2	2
Articles in journals	4	8	20	15
Drug firm literature	14	18	6	4
Drug firm representatives	54	30	20	10
Recommendation from consultants	11	15	33	49
Professional contacts with other doctors	5	12	5	9
Drug firm meetings	–	3	–	–
Other sources	7	12	13	8
Don't know	4	2	1	3
	100	100	100	100
Base	152	263	427	432
All drug firm sources	69	51	28	16
All professional sources	20	35	58	73

Source: Sainsbury, *op. cit.*, pp. 135–40.

Report, show in different ways that GPs regarded medical representatives as the best method of 'finding out about the *existence* of new medicines'. Significantly, however, both show that when it comes to 'finding out about the *efficacy* of new medicines' they prefer to rely on journals and on recommendations from consultants rather than on commercial sources. This suggests that GPs rely on promotion to make them aware that new medicines have become available, but that they do not naively accept company claims without also referring to impartial sources of advise. Table 6.3, also from the Sainsbury Report, throws further light on this subject. It shows that for two therapies, Ultralanum and Mogadon, the firms' representatives had been more influential than consultants in influencing doctors to prescribe. However, for two others, Indocid and Lasix, the opinions of consultants had been overwhelmingly more influential than the firms' representatives. It appears that a family doctor may often decide which relatively safe and simple ointment or sleeping tablet to prescribe on the basis of what the

Table 6.4. Percentages of doctors considering each communication media to be the most important for new medicines and established medicines respectively (base 398 doctors)

Communication	Percentage recording most important for NEW medicines	Percentage recording most important for ESTABLISHED medicines
Medical journal advertisements	5	2
Medical journal articles	17	19
Mailings	4	4
Medical representatives	33	16
MIMS	7	23
ABPI Data Sheet Compendium	1	3
Consultant recommendation	16	12
Other doctors	4	9
Manufacturers' meetings	9	5
Other meetings	3	4
Medical cassette	1	2
Don't know	–	2

Source: Market Investigations Ltd. (1975).

representative has told him; but for an anti-inflammatory or a diuretic the doctor will most often wait for the advice of a consultant.

Table 6.4 has been constructed from answers to questions on a similar theme in the 1975 survey. In this case GPs were asked which of various sources of information they considered most important first for new medicines and then for established medicines. The results provide strong indirect corroboration of the earlier findings. Once again doctors reported that they normally relied on representatives to learn about new medicines, and it seems likely that, as in the earlier survey, they were thinking in this context primarily about discovering the existence of these recent introductions. For established medicines on the other hand, they mentioned consultants and other doctors more often than representatives as a source of information. This corresponds to the conclusions in the Sainsbury Survey that GPs rely on professional colleagues more than representatives to learn about efficacy.

None of these findings are inconsistent with each other but they do not fit in with the Sainsbury conclusion that the industry's representatives were ignorant and irresponsible. That conclusion was based on Table 6.5 which relates to the representative's competence and the accuracy with which he presents his information. Table 6.5, however, breaks one fundamental rule of good market research: avoid the leading question.

> No responsible market researcher will ever deliberately include such questions . . . (if he does) without realising it (this) renders the results of the investigation invalid. It is, therefore, best always to link up the positive with negative, even if the question does not then sound so well. Thus it is not enough to ask: 'Do you like cauliflower?' because this already contains the suggestion that the answer to it should be yes. The question should be put: 'Do you like cauliflower or do you not like cauliflower?'[4]

The inference from this quotation by Max Adler is that the Sainsbury researchers were 'irresponsible', or their results in Table 6.5 are 'invalid'. In the 1975 Market Investigations Survey the same topics were covered in a more neutral fashion. A seven-point scale was used and the results are detailed in Table 6.6; 60 per cent of the sample of GPs felt that the thoroughness of the information provided by representatives fell midway between the extremes of being too much or insufficient. With respect to accuracy of the information provided and knowledge of

Table 6.5. General practitioners' views on the quality of information from drug-firm representatives

Frequency with which the general practitioner thought:	Quality of information from drug-firm representatives In the last year have you ever felt that a representative had insufficient knowledge to tell you what you wanted to know about a product	In the last year have you ever felt that a representative made less of the side-effects of a product he was promoting than was clinically justified?	In the last year have you ever felt that a representative claimed more uses for a product than was clinically justified?
	Per cent	Per cent	Per cent
Very often or fairly often	21	31	35
Not very often	30	27	27
Not at all	49	42	38
	100	100	100

Source: Sainsbury, *op. cit.*, p. 152.

Table 6.6. Attitudes towards three aspects of the medical representative and his behaviour (base for answers: 377 general practitioners) shown in percentages on a seven-point scale

Thoroughness of information						Insufficient
Too much						
3	2	10	69	5	2	1
Accuracy of description						
Accurate						Distorted
41	21	10	18	2	1	1
Knowledge of representative						
Well informed						Not well informed
48	24	13	8	1	1	1

Source: Market Investigations Ltd. (1975).

the representative, only minorities of the GPs interviewed (4 per cent and 3 per cent respectively) felt that information was distorted or was provided by ill-informed representatives, with even smaller minorities (1 per cent in each case) taking the most extreme view. In contrast 72 per cent and 85 per cent respectively felt that representatives tended towards accuracy in their information and had well-informed levels of knowledge. Of these figures 41 per cent and 48 per cent of the sample chose the extreme points on the scale.

Thus it seems clear that representatives, who account for around half of the industry's promotional expenditure, provide useful and reliable information. But doctors do not depend exclusively on representatives, nor indeed on industry sources alone. The Sainsbury questionnaire elicited a misleading conclusion and provided critics with ammunition to use against the industry. If the wrong policy conclusions are drawn as a consequence (such as curtailing promotional expenditure) this may result in the medical profession being deprived of prescribing information which it, the profession, wants. This, in turn, as we shall discuss below, will affect the welfare of the patient, possibly in an adverse manner.

FREEDOM OF SPEECH AND PRESCRIPTION

Prior to his announcement in 1977 that promotion levels would have to be restricted to 10 per cent of sales by 1979 for PPRS purposes, David

Ennals announced in July 1976 that he intended to place a selective ban on pharmaceutical advertising. Only advertising in 'approved' journals would be permitted for the calculation of profits under the PPRS. The DHSS would explicitly have a 'black-list' of medical journals, advertising in which would be disallowed. Mr. Ennals said, 'I intend, however, to do what I can to protect the interests of journals such as the *Lancet*, the *British Medical Journal* and *The Practitioner*.'

The intention of the government to evaluate journals by editorial content would, of course, have been a serious threat to press freedom. To quote Dr. Michael O'Donnel, editor of *World Medicine*, 'there is only one useful classification of medical journals: good journals which are journals which people read, and bad journals which people do not.' Mr. Ennals' dangerously autocratic intention to discriminate between periodicals and to give some preference at the expense of others was dropped in June 1977. But it was only abandoned in exchange for the industry agreeing to attempt to reduce overall promotion levels to 10 per cent of sales by 1979.[5] It was not abandoned because the Minister had come to view the proposal as an infringement on what, in some countries with written Constitutions, would be regarded as unconstitutional, namely interference with the freedom of the press and curtailment of freedom of speech.

The logical complement to controlling or restricting the information which a plurality of firms can provide to doctors is for government to provide prescribing information from a central source. The principle of qualitatively classifying the products of the industry in an attempt to control prescribing is as old as the NHS. In 1949 the Joint Committee on Prescribing was set up to:

> Consider and report from time to time whether it is desirable and practicable to resist or discourage the prescribing by practitioners . . . of:
>
> (1) Drugs and medicines of doubtful value or unethical character; and, (2) unnecessarily expensive brands of standard drugs.

The Committee defined six classifications of drugs of varying degrees of desirability. By 1953 the Committee had classified all then available drugs and recommended the setting up of a smaller standing committee to add new products as they became available.

The Standing Joint Committee on the Classification of Proprietary Preparations (the Cohen Committee) was set up in 1954. Basically, the classification system permitted doctors freedom of prescription (categories '*N* and *P*') of non-standard drugs for which there was evidence of therapeutic value. Prescribing of drugs of unproven value was discouraged (categories *O* and *H*), alone or in combination with approved drugs. Under category *S* the prescribing of branded equivalents of standard drugs, of other combinations, or of medicines only slightly varying from standard was also discouraged. 'Standard' meant those drugs listed in publications such as the British National Formulary (BNF).

Discouragement' took two main forms. The Committee agreed that there should be 'no absolute restrictions' on the doctor's freedom to prescribe for his individual patient's needs but that if his overall cost of prescribing was being investigated then he might be called on to justify his prescriptions in categories *O*, *H* and *S*. Further, category *S* drugs should only be prescribable if a price had been agreed for the products between the Ministry and the manufacturer. To apply this 'discouragement' the VPRS was developed. Embodied in the doctor's terms of employment are conditions stipulating that remuneration may be withheld if excessively costly prescribing is proved. Each GP receives an annual statement showing his prescription costs, the average for his area and for the country. If his are substantially above average he may receive a visit from a Regional Medical Officer who will discuss his prescribing with him. (In England and Wales 3,000 such visits were paid in 1972.)[6] If his costs are deemed excessive the case may be referred to the Local Medical Committee who are empowered to withhold remuneration. Only one such reference was made in 1972, and the doctor had £50 withheld from his salary.

In 1964 the Cohen Committee was wound up and reconstituted under the chairmanship of Professor MacGregor. This reconstruction was brought about by the removal of some of Cohen's functions to the newly-established Committee on Safety of Drugs and by the growing feeling that the Cohen classifications were somewhat confusing.

The MacGregor Committee was set up with the following terms of reference:

> To advise on the classification of proprietary pharmaceutical preperations with the object of helping doctors to decide which should be used in the treatment of their patients, and to identify *those* preparations the prescribing of which appears to call for special justification.

In 1965 the Committee published its system of classification. The Committee recommended freedom of prescription for its first four categories and discouragement for its last two. Briefly, MacGregor categories *M* and *A*1 contained standard drugs, or those non-standard drugs with little or no therapeutic difference from standard equivalents. Categories *A*2 and *A*3 contained preparations which could be recommended for use but which were considered unacceptable due to lack of proven efficacy or excess toxicity.

The public face of the Committee was its periodical publication *Proplist* which contained details of all the preparations. *Proplist* was circulated to each doctor.

Whether or not MacGregor had much of an effect on prscribing is an open question. 'Doctrinaire' was a term frequently used of the Committee's attitudes, particularly towards combination products. The ABPI on requesting pointers to the Committee's overall policy received little satisfaction in reply. 'Apart from indicating certain combinations of drugs which it considers not good medical practice to prescribe, the Committee does not feel it possible to give more precise guidance.'[7]

What is not often pointed out is that hazards can occur when dependence is placed on advice from a single official source as opposed to plural, commercially competing sources of prescribing information. There are two main hazards. First, there is an inevitable tendency for centralised and official sources of information to represent an establishment view. Thus attempts to persuade an official committee to advocate the use of a new medicine can become a battle against conservatism. A case which illustrates this arose when the manufacturers of the tetracyclines started to promote their use as prophylactics against acute exacerbations in chronic bronchitics during the winter season. In November 1954 the government-sponsored publication *Prescribers' Notes* stated categorically that oxytetracycline and cholortetracycline were 'not indicated' in chronic chest infections. The manufacturers were severely criticised for their promotion. Thus, if *Prescribers' Notes* had been the primary channel of prescribing advice to doctors, the tetracyclines would never have been widely used in chronic bronchitis and no one, including the official 'experts' would ever have had an opportunity to assess their value in such cases in practice. Dogmatic opposition to their use would probably have remained unchallenged. In fact, the companies rode out the criticisms and continued to promote their antibiotics for this indication. Prescribers accepted the evidence advanced by the companies; tetracyclines continued to be prescribed for chronic bronchitis; and as their use became more widespread they were seen to be of considerable value. In the light of this experience, *Prescribers' Journal*, which had by then succeeded the earlier *Prescribers' Notes*, stated in May 1961 that 'probably the largest consumption of tetracyclines in Britain is in patients which chronic bronchitis where the infection is often due to a mixture of bacteria. Here the tetracyclines are undoubtedly valuable.' By October 1969 *Prescribers' Journal* stated, just as categorically as its predecessor had expressed the opposite view 15 years earlier, that the tetracyclines were 'probably the antibiotics of first choice' for the treatment of chronic bronchitis. Neither the antibiotics nor the nature of the infection had changed between 1954 and 1969. All that had changed was the established medical opinion on their usefulness.

To the observer, it would appear that the knowledge to lay down guidelines for choice is not yet sufficiently available to preclude subjective judgements. Propagating the views of one school of thought in such a situation may not be appropriate. The dangers of such uniformity were succinctly put by *The Economist:* 'If anyone disputes this let him ask himself why a middle-class generation, born between the wars, has grown up without its tonsils or its foreskin.[8]

This lesson has apparently been learned. *Proplist* and the Committee responsible for its publication were stood down in 1968.

Second, reliance on centralised sources of information would tend to favour the first medicine to be introduced with a particular type of pharmacological action, and would tend to discount subsequent marginal advances or apparent duplicates. Officialdom is unlikely to endorse, far less recommend, an apparent copy. Yet many of the most important therapeutic advances have come about via the route of minor molecular manipulations which at first sight seem to be clinically identical to existing products. For example, in a reference to the development of hydrocostisone by adding two hydrogen atoms to the original cortisone the Nobel Laureate in Physiology and Medicine, Phillip Hench, stated that this 'raises the effect of the electrolytes many, many times. And, if we were to ask the pharmaceutical chemist not to bother with minor modifications on the drawing board, we might miss some of the most amazing, hopeful cortisones that have ever been discovered.'[9] By extension, a drug firm which is not permitted to promote a 'minor modification' will 'not bother' to develop it.

QUALITY CONTROL

A brand name, known to a prescriber by its promotional back-up, provides an implicit guarantee of quality. Unsatisfactory brands can be avoided and selection of products with the desired qualities is facilitated. Branding is an important practice in the industry; in 1965 88.8 per cent by value of all NHS prescriptions were written out for products available only under a brand name.[10]

The Sainsbury Report suggested two major advantages to be expected if brand names were prohibited, first, more effective price competition would result; and, second, a source of confusion due to a multiplicity of names for the same drug would be removed. Confusion due to a proliferation of different brand names for the same product is more illusory than real, however. In 1965 within the total of 2403 brands listed in *Medinex* there were 2177 different chemical formulations: an average of only 1.1 brand names per formulation which can hardly be termed a confusing multiplicity of names for the same products.[11] The emergence, *ceteris paribus*, of a greater degree of price-competition if branding were to disappear is, of course, indisputable. The crucial question is to assess the value of the benefits accruing to the community from this competition. The Public Accounts Committee attempted to measure these benefits in 1964–65. The Ministry of Health provided the PAC with evidence that if all drugs were prescribed generically then in only twenty-five cases would there be a possible saving in price due to a branded drug being dearer than its standard equivalent. In all other cases the branded drug was either the only version available, or it was itself cheaper than the non-branded duplicate. Of these twenty-five drugs, three had had prices agreed under the Voluntary Price Regulation Scheme; and if a switch in prescribing had taken place from the remaining twenty-two to generic products only, in 1964 this would have resulted in a total saving to the NHS of just over £83,000.[12]

Against the advantages to be gained from discouraging brand names must be placed the advantages provided by branding. Principally, these are primarily associated with indentification of the product. To avoid circular reasoning, these will only hold when duplication of product is present. (Duplication is present, in individual cases, to a greater degree than the average ratio of 1.1 brands per formulation would suggest.) If a particular brand is known to be satisfactory, the doctor can prescribe with confidence, and with the knowledge that his patient will receive a specific therapeutic agent. Generic prescribing may result in the same agent being dispensed, but there is no guarantee of this.

Differences in manufacturing technique and in form of presentation often induce differing physiological responses in the same patient from the same medicine. The *British Medical Journal* stated that 'there is a mistaken belief that the active constituent, to which the official name only refers, constitues the sole basis for a drug's effectiveness. This is by no means always the case; the physiological response to a drug may also be a function of its pharmaceutical formulation.'[13]

This raises the issue of bioavailability, namely the rate at which a drug becomes available for absorption in the patient. This can vary with particle size, salt form, diluent, lubricant, compression of tablet and type of capsule. The more sophisticated the formulation, as in sustained release preparations or enteric coated forms, the more variables there are which affect the absorption rate. A further difficulty is the fact that conditions of absorption, metabolism and excretion may change with the disease process, and may not be the same in each patient for every day he takes the drug. Beckett points out that some of the most widely used antibiotics, steroids and anti-inflammatory agents (among many others) vary significantly, in therapeutic terms, one brand from the other, while still being regarded chemically and generically as 'equivalents'.[14]

The opponents of brand-name prescribing suggest that the advantages could be retained and the disadvantages removed if brand names were abolished and the doctor prescribed generically adding, if he wished, the name of the desired manufacturer to the prescription form. Sainsbury in fact expressly states that it is 'important that the manufacturer . . . be easily identified and that the doctor should be able to ensure . . . (that he is) the maker of his choice'.[15] The sincerity of this last remark is questionable. Intuitively, it seems quite improbable that time-pressed doctors, who write out several dozen prescriptions per day, would even consider adding the desired manufacturer's name to the prescription. This appears even less likely when it is remembered that generic prescribing will in some cases entail still extra wording to specify presentation form.

If this is so, then the comment quoted above would appear to be merely a verbal sop to those lobbying for retention of brand names. On the other hand, if doctors would indeed prescribe on a large scale by manufacturer, it can be postulated that, far from promoting more effective price competition, rather more rigid and long-lasting monopoly situations would result. Currently, drug firms' promotional emphasis is predominantly on the brand advertised. Since the average life of a drug is short, the average length of brand-name-induced monopoly is also relatively short. When the drug disappears from the market, so too does any monopoly position it may have provided. If, however, brand names were to disappear and doctors were to be expected to prescribe by manufacturer, then a massive switch of promotional tactics might take place. The stress might well shift from product names to company names. In such a situation, any monopoly position or market preference created by unique name advertising would not wither away with the demise of a product superseded by a more advanced one but would last for as long as the firm cared to retain the position.

Moreover, under such circumstances, barriers to entry would be relatively higher. An innovating company previously unknown in the market would be at a marked disadvantage to a similarly placed firm which had built up a considerable goodwill to its house name. Doctors are used to having to assess the value of new drugs introduced under unique brand names. They are not, except in a few cases, very familiar with company names. Currently an entrant firm merely has to promote the brand name of its entrant product: a task almost equal in magnitude to that of most drug firms introducing a new product. If company names become as familiar to doctors as brand names are now, a potential entrant would have the additional barrier to overcome of inducing doctors to shift from existing, known company names.

DIFFUSION OF INNOVATION

It is now well established that promotion is significantly associated with innovation in the industry. Figure 6.1 shows that while relatively new medicines are by no means the only ones promoted, recent innovations are regarded as the products requiring the greatest intensity of marketing back-up. Once a product has gained acceptance, there is still a need for some advertising of the reminder type. Doctors, like any other human 'buyers', 'do not have perfect memories; nor are they a static body: there are continually new potential recruits to be drawn from the newly employed . . . familiar products are from time to time improved or adapted to different purposes, and the manufacturer must make known their new look'.[16] Figure 6.1 indicates the comparative steadiness of reminder advertising on a product after it is accepted by the market. The average expenditure in the first two months of 1965 on

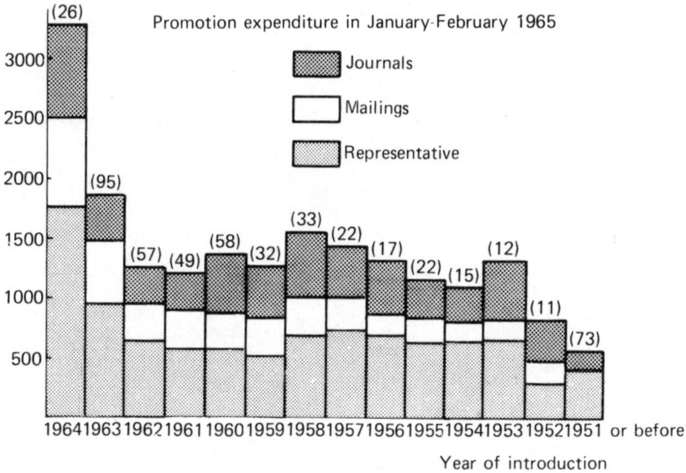

(No. of products promoted shown in brackets)

Fig. 6.1. Promotional expenditure per product promoted by age of product.

Source: G. Teeling-Smith, *Economics and Innovation in the Pharmaceutical Industry* (Office of Health Economics, 1968, p. 65.)

products introduced between 1953 and 1962 varied only from £1500 to £1100 in the period of examination.

Figure 6.2 confirms the need for a high initial level of promotion to obtain doctor-acceptance for a new product. It might be expected that those therapeutic markets with greater numbers of new products would also be subject to greater promotional activity. Figure 6.2 is a simple exercise carried out to test this relationship.

As can be seen from an inspection of the diagram, one therapeutic grouping, antibiotics, was *ceteris paribus* spending a disproportionate sum on promotion relative to the remainder of the industry. Removing antibiotics from the study ($n = 37$ becomes $n = 36$) the coefficient of determination, r^2, rises from 0.72 to 0.83 ($r = 0.91$). Thus while it could be suggested that innovation is a principal determinant of promotion in most groupings, in the antibiotics market, which alone accounts for over 20 per cent of industry sales to the NHS, other factors are of much greater importance in determining promotional levels. It may be that antibiotic promotion was unnecessarily and monopolistically high. Another explanation is that it was wastefully high, not from mono-

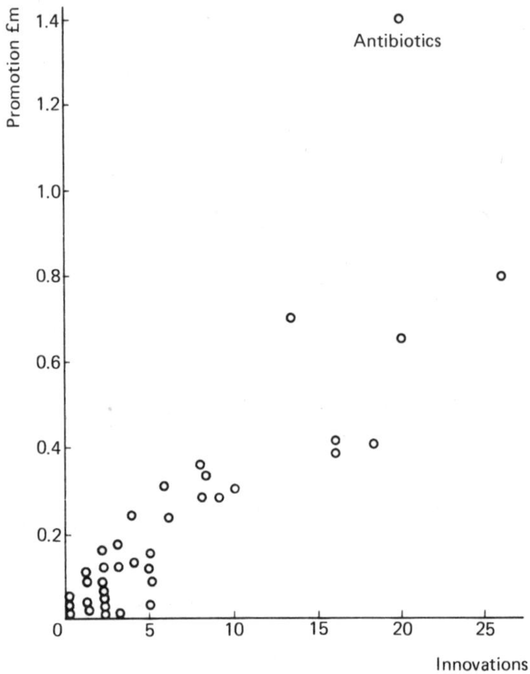

Fig. 6.2. Therapeutic classes, promotion 1966, innovations 1962–65. *Source:* W. Duncan Reekie, 'Some Problems Associated with the Marketing of Ethical Pharmaceutical Products', *Journal of Industrial Economics* (1970).

polistic or non-competitive reasons, but because the industry was having to advertise heavily to counter the mis-information provided by government (in the years under study) relating to the use of the tetracyclines in bronchitis. As was noted above, it took from 1954 to 1969 for official publications to move from a position antagonistic to their use, to one favouring them.

In the USA similar relationships have been discovered. Telser's finding that industry entry is significantly associated with promotion was discussed in Chapter 5, and inferred from Fig. 5.1. Telser tested the hypothesis that high promotional outlays constitute a barrier to entry by cementing prescriber loyalties to existing firms or brands. If that is so then an inverse association between the two should exist. Telser split his seventeen sub-market sample into two time periods, 1963–68 and 1968–72. In only three instances did the change in promotional

Table 6.7. Diffusion of benefits for three major drug innovations

	(1) Actual loss from disease as percent of loss expected without drug			(2) Saving from drug as percent of tenth-year saving		
	(a)	(b)	(c)	(a)	(b)	(c)
Years after introduction of drug	Polio (paralytic cases)[a]	TB (deaths)[b]	Mental hospital stay (patient-days)[c]	Polio	TB	Mental hospital
1	59	93	98	41	11	5
2	31	86	94	69	22	15
3	10	77	86	90	36	35
4	14	72	76	86	44	60
5	22	59	79	78	64	53
6	9	48	81	91	81	48
7	3	41	75	97	92	63
8	2	39	67	98	95	83
9	1	37	67	99	99	83
10	nil	36	61	100	100	100

[a] Actual number of new paralytic cases of polio reported in each year (1956–64), divided by the number of cases expected if Salk vaccine had not been introduced. Expected cases for 1955–61 estimated in American Medical Association, *Report of the Commission on the Cost of Medical Care*, III (1964); the 1961 estimate is used for 1962–64.

[b] Actual death-rate from tuberculosis in each year, 1948–57, divided by 1947 rate x exp – 0.045 x number of years from 1947. This exponent is the average annual decline of the TB death-rate from 1920 to 1947 which, it is presumed, would have continued in the absence of any drug innovation.

[c] Patient-days in mental hospitals per new admittee in each year, 1955–64, divided by 800, which approximates the level prevailing in the decade prior to introduction of chlorpromazine.

Source: Peltzman, in Helms, *op. cit.*, p. 20.

intensity have an opposite sign to the change in entry; in one case entry decreased with no change in promotion; in the remaining thirteen markets the change in promotional intensity was of the same sign as the change in entry. The two tend to move in the same direction. Promotion is not a barrier to entry, it is a means to the launch and successful diffusion of innovation.

Even if resources are apparently wasted when expenditure is unnecessarily high, in a highly innovative industry it may be better to bear some waste than to suffer the costs of low diffusion of information and persuasion. In the Soviet Union promotion of new drugs is undertaken by the Health Ministry, not by the industry. Information about new drugs is usually restricted to mailed literature or journal articles. The information is frequently overlooked,[17] forgotten or ignored by the Soviet practitioner. It is neither prompt enough, voluminous enough, nor is there a sufficiently strong persuasive element, to encourage the doctor to use the new advances. The result is a substantial lag between the introduction of a new medicine and incremental benefits by the patient.

Professor Sam Peltzman[18] attempted to measure the benefits that might have accrued to society (in the USA) had diffusion been more rapid in the case of two major drug innovations, TB drugs and tranquilisers. Peltzman made conservative assumptions in his estimates. He focused only on mortality effects, not morbidity effects, for TB drugs. In the case of tranquilisers he ignored the impact on emotional well being and economic productivity of patients treated outside hospital and concentrated only on mental hospital admissions. In both cases he assumed that all benefits would be achieved by society within ten years of innovation, irrespective of rate of diffusion. This too is modest. The TB drugs were introduced in the late 1940s, yet even in the 1970s the decline in the year-on-year death rate from TB is still almost double the pre-innovation decline. Similarly, although tranquilisers first made their impact on length of patient confinement in 1954, this decline has not yet run its course.

Table 6.7 indicates Peltzman's estimates of the benefits that might be attained from faster diffusion within a decade of new product launch. Column (1) of the table expresses the observed toll from a disease as a percentage of what could have been expected without the drug in each of the ten years after innovation. In column (2) the implied saving in each year is expressed as a percentage of the tenth-year saving, the presumed maximum.

Table 6.8 is an attempt to put the benefits of more rapid diffusion into

Table 6.8. Potential gain from more rapid diffusion, TB drugs and tranquilisers

Years after introduction of drug	TB drugs (lives saved, in thousands)[a]	Tranquilisers (patient-days saved, in millions)[b]
1	13.1	78
2	19.2	119
3	21.5	117
4	15.8	58
5	4.9	50
6	3.2	90
7	1.9	70
8	0.8	29
9	0.2	34
Total	80.6	645

[a] A hypothetical TB death-rate series is computed by assuming a diffusion pattern for savings equal to that for polio vaccine in column 2(a), Table 6.7. The difference between the observed series and the hypothetical series is multiplied by 211 million, the 1973 US population, to get the potential saving in lives on the current population base.

[b] A hypothetical series of average length of stay per new mental hospital admittee is derived by assuming a diffusion pattern for reduction of this figure equal to that for polio vaccine. The difference between the observed series (365 x average daily census in mental hospitals in year/new admissions that year) and the hypothetical series is multiplied by 700,000, the approximate number of 1973 mental-hospital admissions, to get the potential saving in patient-days on a current basis.

Source: Ibid., p. 22.

some meaningful nontext. There the benefits from TB drugs and tranquilisers are estimated on the assumption that they diffused as rapidly as the Salk polio vaccine (*see* Table 6.7). The Salk vaccine received the benefits of extensive America-wide publicity after a clinical trial involving 500,000 children. Within two years of the end of the trial 75 per cent of the population under twenty had received at least one dose of the drug. Even if only a fraction of the savings suggested by Table 6.8 had been attained the gross benefits would have been huge. Peltzman suggests that if one considers only the added earnings of potential TB victims in present value terms of, say, $50,000 per life, then the present value at year of innovation of more rapid diffusion of TB drugs would have been $3 billion. For the tranquilisers Peltzman obtains estimated savings of $9 billion by calculating savings in hospitalisation costs alone (ignoring productivity increases from shorter patient confinements). He concludes: 'By way of comparison, gains of this order once per decade could easily pay for a *doubling* of current drug promotion expenses, if that is what it takes to realise them' (italics added).

7 Politics and Research

R & D EXPENDITURE

Research and development expenditure by the UK pharmaceutical industry in 1976 reached an estimate £100 million. This figure is large in absolute terms but is given some sense of proportion from the fact that it now takes up to 10–12 years to bring a major new medicine through all the development stages prior to marketing — at a cost of £10–£15 million per product.

Table 7.1 shows the pattern of growth of the industry's R & D. expenditure over the past 24 years. Similar growth rates have been achieved by other countries' drug industries. The UK is among the largest spenders. International monetary comparisons tend to give a misleading picture of relative R & D efforts, however. Exchange rate fluctuations and salary purchasing power differentials distort casual inferences. A more realistic measure of comparable R & D effort is that of manpower. The US industry is by far the largest in terms of personnel

Table 7.1. R & D expenditure by the British pharmaceutical industry

Year	*£m*	*Year*	*£m*
1953	2.8	1964	10.4
1954	3.0	1965	11.6
1955	3.5	1966	13.0
1956	3.9	1967*	14.5
1957	4.2	1970*	22.0
1958	5.1	1971*	24.0
1959	6.3	1972*	27.0
1960	7.5	1973	44.1
1961	7.8	1974*	50.0
1962	8.3	1975*	70.0
1963	na	1976*	100.0

*Estimated

Source: ABPI surveys.

Table 7.2. R & D personnel employed by local pharmaceutical industries (1975)

Italy	4700
France	6000
Japan	7300
Switzerland	5000
UK	9500
West Germany	15,000
USA	22,000

Source: P.M.A.

employed on R & D (Table 7.2) — almost as big in aggregate as the UK and Germany combined.

The Pharmaceutical Manufacturers' Association (PMA) of America surveys most leading firms to find what disease groups they are focusing on in their research. The most prominent are (Table 7.3) infectious diseases; cardiovascular diseases; hypertension; mental and nervous disorders; arthritis and related diseases; asthma; dermatologic conditions; allergies and, of course, cancer. These are among the most

Table 7.3. US Applied R & D expenditures, pharmaceuticals, by product class (1975)

Product class	Share of R & D dollar 1975 %
Anti-ineffective	20.1
Central nervous system and sense organs	18.0
Neoplasms, endocrine system and metabolic diseases	15.5
Cardiovasculars	14.9
Respiratory	5.5
Gastrointestinal and genitourinary system	5.1
Biologicals	3.0
Dermatologicals	2.8
Diagnostics	1.2
Vitamins	1.1
Other	5.9
Veterinary preparations	6.5
Veterinary biologicals	0.4
	100.0

prevalent health problems facing the world today, and consequently where the commercial rewards for successful R & D effort are highest. Research investment is consequently aimed at the areas with the greatest potential returns in both monetary and social terms.

ECONOMIC ANALYSIS AND R & D

The debate surrounding the topic of market structure is intimately connected with the relationship between R & D and size of firm. The proposed merger between Beecham and Glaxo was turned down by the Monopolies Commission primarily because of the adverse effects it might have on pharmaceutical R & D in the UK. The controversy has two main facets. First, whether or not larger firms perform proportionately more R & D than smaller ones. Second, whether or not larger R & D efforts produce proportionately more innovations.

R & D is an absolutely expensive activity and it is presumed that firms must be of some minimum size in order to undertake a meaningful effort. The NEDO study of the industry suggested that in 1970 terms the smallest R & D effort, based on at least three projects, would cost a minimum of £½ million. Possibly a budget of nearer £2 million is required in order to support a full range of skills and facilities and to provide some insurance against failure. Those who argue that larger firms conduct proportionately more R & D do so on the basis that larger firms (*a*) have greater resources and (*b*) have a greater degree of market power that can be used to generate an absolutely higher level of profits from any resulting innovation. This is a familiar argument and has been with us at least since Schumpeter first wrote of the 'Perennial Gate of Creative Destruction'.[1] Disagreement arises not over the need to have some degree of size and market power to encourage R & D activity, but over whether or not an increase in market power and size above such a threshold would result in a relatively complacent large firm whose urge to engage in the risks of innovative activity would be relatively less. For example, referring to the Beecham–Glaxo merger proposal the Monopolies Commission wrote:

> Beecham's research interests are relatively narrow, as is also the range of drugs which it sells. The prosperity of such a company is . . . vulnerable . . . (and it has) in consequence, a strong incentive to remedy its potential weakness by broadening the scope of its research. Should Beecham acquire Glaxo . . . the resulting company

Table 7.4. Summary of the case for an association between market structure and innovation

Arguments in favour of high concentration	Major reservations
(*A*) *Cost of resources*. Market control raises profitability and reduces the demands on management, thus implying a lower opportunity cost of resources devoted to R & D. (*B*) *Risk*. Reduced short-run price competition provides greater security and permits a longer time horizon for research.	There may be financial advantages *for enterprising firms*, but the opportunities may not be realised if the incentive to innovate is impaired (see *C*–*E* below). Further, the relevance of financial advantages may vary with the scale of the technology.
(*C*) *Competitive incentives*. The risk of retaliation discourages oligopolistic price competition. Non-price competition is thereby encouraged, being less readily matched by competitors.	Non-price competition may give way to collusion unless the technology offers large gains from innovation. If one firm can appropriate these gains, the initial market structure may be irrelevant.
(*D*) *Market share incentives*. A large market share implies a greater absolute gain from any given proportionate change in costs or revenues. Therefore the costs of R & D are more easily recovered.	(i) Market leaders may gain less if new products replace existing products. (ii) Monopolists may bias the choice of innovations so as to preserve their dominance.
(*E*) *Risk of imitation*. Market dominance reduces the risk of imitation by competitors, and enables market leaders to retain the benefits of innovations.	Given that dominant firms may seek to delay innovations competing with established products, they may prefer a 'fast second' strategy, using market dominance to take over the proven innovations of smaller competitors.
(*F*) *Size of firm*. *A*–*E* above may be reinforced if the monopolists or oligopolists are also large firms. Potential benefits include: (*a*) Indivisible innovations may require an absolutely large volume of resources. (*b*) Economies of scale may exist in the R & D process if	The benefits of size may be exaggerated. Reservations include: (i) Large firms may stifle creativity, and restrict invention and discovery. (ii) Advantages of size are more significant for development than for research, and may vary between industries. (iii) If there are no economies of scale in the R & D process, small firms

Table 7.4. Continued

Arguments in favour of high concentration	Major reservations
specialised staff or equipment are required. Large firms are then more able to finance the optimum scale. (*c*) Economies of scale in marketing or production may enable large firms to exploit innovations more profitably. (*d*) The risk of failure of an R & D programme may be reduced if the number of independent projects in that programme can be increased. (*e*) Large firms may have a more diversified product range, giving more scope for the internal exploitation of new discoveries.	with lower overheads may be more cost-effective and more flexible. (iv) Many small firms do no R & D. The owner-managers of those which do may be more highly motivated and less risk-averse than the salaried managers of large firms. (v) Diversification may encourage basic research, but is less relevant for targetted R & D. If there are economies of scale in R & D, a diversified firm may dissipate its resources over too wide an area.

Source: R. W. Shaw and C. J. Sutton, *Industry and Competition* (Macmillan, 1976) p. 203.

> would be much less vulnerable . . . and some of the research which Beecham might otherwise have done . . . might not be undertaken.[2]

The second facet of the controversy, whether larger R & D efforts are more productive, is, of course, merely a restatement, in the R & D situation, of the question as to when, if at all, scale economies are exhausted. The *a priori* case for and against the existence of diseconomies of scale in R & D is even more indefinable than in the manufacturing area. R & D productivity depends to a considerable extent on individual creativity. Jewkes[3] and his associates have shown that inventive creativity is scattered fairly evenly across the size distribution of organisations. When an invention moves into the stage of applied research and development, however, it is often argued that there is then more scope for the economic advantages of size to result in an overall reduction in unit cost.

It would appear that no definitive case for or against a higher level of concentration in the industry can be made. Economic theory is too imprecise to predict with certainty the strength of any relationship between market structure and innovation. Indeed it is too imprecise to predict even the direction of the relationship. Table 7.4, reproduced from a recent text on the economics of industrial organisation, summarises the arguments in favour of increased concentration and counters these arguments with an equally long list of reservations.

A number of empirical studies have been published in recent years which have examined these areas of dispute. Tables 7.5 and 7.6 summarise the results obtained. Only one study, and that inconclusively, suggests that total R & D effort might increase if the

Table 7.5. Summary of results of studies relating size of firm to R & D efforts

Study	Index of firm size	Index of R & D effort	Conclusions
Grabowski[4]	Sales	R & D expenditure	Research intensity initially increases with firm size, but declines thereafter.
Mansfield[5]	Sales	R & D expenditure	R & D expenditure does not increase more than proportionately with firm size.
Monopolies Commission[6]	Sales	R & D expenditure	The relationship is non-linear. Intensity reaches a maximum below maximum firm size.
Reekie[7]	Sales	R & D expenditure	The relationship is non-linear. Intensity reaches a maximum below maximum firm size.
Schwartzman[8]	Sales	R & D employment (exclusive of auxiliary staff)	R & D effort increases less than proportionately with firm size if a linear logarithmic equation is used. The results are reversed if a quadratic equation is tested.

Source: W. Duncan Reekie, *The Economics of the Pharmaceutical Industry* (Macmillan, 1976), p. 115.

industry were composed of fewer and larger firms. The investigations carried out by Grabowski, Mansfield, this author and the Monopolies Commission all arrive at broadly the same conclusion: the largest pharmaceutical firms, while possibly the biggest absolute performers of R & D, are not the most research-intensive firms.

The studies reported in Table 7.6 differed in their objectives, in their statistical methodology, and in their measures of innovative output. A wholly satisfactory yardstick of innovation has yet to be devised. However, the range of indices employed in Table 7.6 does cover most of the parameters generally thought of as indicators of the value of a new medicine to society. Despite the employment of so many different measures of R & D success the studies by Comanor, Grabowski, the Monopolies Commission, this author, and by Schnee all fall into a common pattern. All suggest the presence of diseconomies of scale in pharmaceutical R & D Angilley, however, discovered constant returns to scale. And Schwartzman, reproducing (with certain statistical differences) most of the previous studies, came to the very opposite conclusion, that economies of scale are important.

How can these differences be reconciled? If one ignores the intricacies and technicalities of econometric debate, then the most obvious differences between Angilley and Schwartzman and the earlier studies is in the time periods which the two groups cover. The Angilley and Schwartzman studies are restricted to the second half of the 1960s. The others are predominantly or exclusively dependent on data relating to years prior to this period.

This may be significant and may indicate changing circumstances in pharmaceutical R & D It has already been pointed out that the real costs of R & D are rising. This was attributable to two factors. The remaining unconquered disease areas provide relatively difficult technological problems. Second, the costs of meeting the requirements for new drug registration, both in the UK and overseas, have risen dramatically. Both are phenomena of the 1960s. They may be responsible for the apparent contradictions evident in Tables 7.5 and 7.6 Certainly a dogmatic stance cannot be taken with regard to the presence or absence of scale economies in R & D

Finally, there is the more general issue that success in pharmaceutical research depends primarily on the ability to generate promising novel ideas. Given the serendipitous nature of much pharmaceutical R & D it would seem from a nationalistic viewpoint that the current small number of British-owned research centres in the UK should not be further reduced. Such a reduction might merely lead to fewer different

Table 7.6. Summary of results of studies relating size of R & D effort to innovative output

Study	Index of R & D effort	Index of R & D output	Period covered by study	Conclusions
Angilley[10]	R & D Expenditure	New compounds (a) weighted by market success (b) weighted by degree of therapeutic advance	1958–70	'No strong deviation from constant returns to scale exists'
Comanor[9]	Professional research personnel	First 24 months sales of new single entities	1955–60	'Substantial diseconomies of scale in R & D encountered even by moderately sized firms'
Grabowski[4]	Professional research personnel	Patents	1959–62	Large firms do not necessarily have higher research productivity than smaller
Monopolies Commission[6]	Size of firm gauged by sales	Major pharmaceutical innovations	1950–71	Largest firms were responsible for a disproportionately small number of innovations

Reekie[7]	R & D expenditure	Patents	1959–66	Firms below the largest size were not only the most research intensive but also among the most successful
Schnee[11]	Size of firm gauged by sales	Major innovations, with or without medical or economic weights	1935–62	'The firms that have contributed the most innovations relative to their size are not the largest firms, but somewhat smaller ones'
Schwartzman[8]	R & D employment (exclusive of auxiliary staff)	(a) New entities	1965–70	'Economies of scale are large'
		(b) New entities weighted by 1972 sales		'Economies of scale are large'
		(c) weighted by Novelty		'Large and increasing economies of scale'
		(d) Weighted by medical importance		'Large and increasing economies of scale'
		(e) Weighted by the number of prescriptions issued in 1971		'Large and increasing economies of scale'
		(f) Patents	1968–70	'Large economies of scale'

Source: Ibid., 116–17.

ideas being pursued in any given field of common interest and so impair the British-owned industry's overall prospects of success in finding and developing new products.

BRITISH AND AMERICAN EVIDENCE SINCE REGULATION TIGHTENED

Additional confirmation for the view that the relationship between firm size and innovative output has altered in recent years is provided in Table 7.7, where the results obtained in a study by Grabowski and Vernon are displayed. Their investigation explicitly compared different time periods. Their findings indicate that the four largest firms in the industry accounted for a share of innovational output from 1957 to 1966 not dissimilar to their share of sales. By 1967–71, however, at 48.7 per cent, their share of innovational output was much greater than their share of total sales. (The long-run implications of this may be disturbing.)

In an attempt to ascertain why the change depicted in Table 7.7 has occurred the (USA) results were compared with those from another country (UK) where the regulatory climate was much less stringent. The authors suggested that the depletion of R & D opportunities would affect the productivity of R & D in all countries in a similar manner. However, any negative effects of regulation would show up as an additional influence in a country with a stiffer regulatory framework. They found, in a comparison between the UK and USA, that in the

Table 7.7. Grabowski and Vernon's estimates of concentration of innovational output in the US ethical drug industry

	Periods		
	1957–61	1962–66	1967–71
Four largest firms' share of innovational output	24.0	25.0	48.7
Four largest firms' share of total sales	26.5	24.0	26.1

Note: Innovational output is measured by NCE sales during the first three full years after product introduction.

Source: H. G. Grabowski and J. M. Vernon, 'Consumer Protection Regulation in Ethical Drugs', *American Economic Review* (1977).

USA R & D productivity declined by about six-fold between 1960–61 and 1966–70. The corresponding decrease in the UK was only half as great. They argue as a consequence that 1962 Amendments to the Food, Drug and Cosmetic Act, by themselves, rougly doubled the cost of producing and introducing an NCE in the USA.

THE DRUG LAG OR HOW THE USA LOST OUT

Parker[12] argues that the atmosphere surrounding the Amendments was one of 'mistrust'. This resulted in the FDA having a role which was intended to delay rather than to 'promote and foster innovation'. In such an atmosphere, delays in approving innovations caused by the regulatory process become a benefit and not a cost in the eyes of those responsible for operating the agency. Congressional criticism of the FDA's final approval of beta blockers for angina underlines the persistence of this mistrust.[13] As one commentator observed, this case '... is destined to become a classic in the history of *political pharmacology*, with very wide implications for the legislation and regulation of drugs'[14] (emphasis added). In most other countries, such ill-informed criticism would never have been voiced. The USA is thus

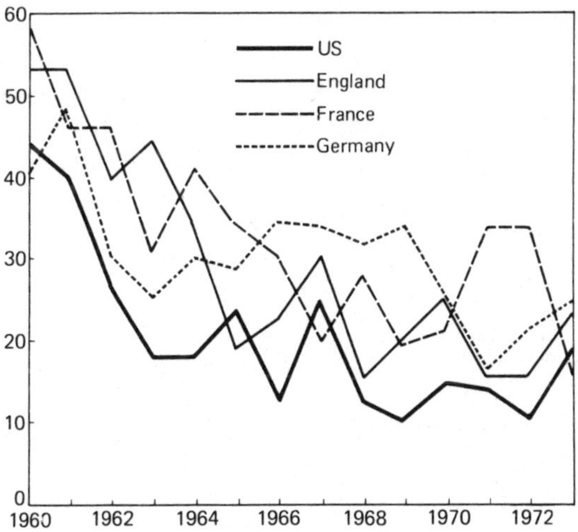

Fig. 7.1. Annual marketing of NCEs in United States, England, France and Germany.

Source: Grabowski, *op. cit.* (1976), p. 20.

saddled with a regulatory system where sound medical judgement may not be the sole criterion guiding decisions. The FDA is involved in an atmosphere that requires political as well as medical caution. This is a pressure that can do little to improve the quality of operations.

Against this background it is useful to examine Fig. 7.1. This shows that the numbers of NCEs launched in four important drug markets fell from 1960 to 1973, and did so particularly sharply after the international introduction of regulations governing safety. The data also show, however, much lower absolute rates of introduction in the USA than elsewhere over the entire period. This is consistent with the view that drug regulation is relatively more stringent in the USA. Moreover, since the USA is the largest single performer of R & D, any reduction in R & D effectiveness in American laboratories will effect the NCE introduction rate elsewhere.

Figure 7.1 is also consistent with the 'depletion of research opportunities' hypothesis. There is, however, a third explanation. Not only can it be argued that NCE launches have declined because of diminishing returns to R & D effort and rising costs due to regulation, it can also be argued that most of the decline is attributable to a rapid fall off in drugs representing little or no therapeutic gain. This is the view of Commissioner Schmidt of the FDA who produced the data on which Fig. 7.2 is based in his evidence to a Senate Sub-Committee in 1974.

This third view has been challenged on several grounds. First, alternative 'expert' ratings have produced non-identical results.[15] This is merely a repetition of the 'battle of the lists' in the 1970s which occurred, as was seen in Chapter 1, during the Kefauver investigations into the industry. Second, a leading economist[16] examined the market's evaluation (*i.e.* prescribing physicians and patients) of NCEs. And third, two well-known academic pharmacologists[17] identified NCEs which were available in the UK and the USA and also named those which were not marketed in the USA due to the very rigid regulatory process in the latter country.

The economist, Professor Sam Pelzman, used a consumer surplus measure of the gains and losses from the amendments. He estimated a demand schedule for NCEs pre- and post-1962. This was then used to calculate the change in consumer surplus attributable to the Amendments. His methodology can be inferred from Fig. 7.3. Consider *ADM* as the pre-1962 demand, and *GHEN* as the post-Amendments demand, both with a ruling price *B*. The latter demand is lower because either effective drugs are no longer marketed due to the Amendments and so demand for them is non-existent, or some innovations are

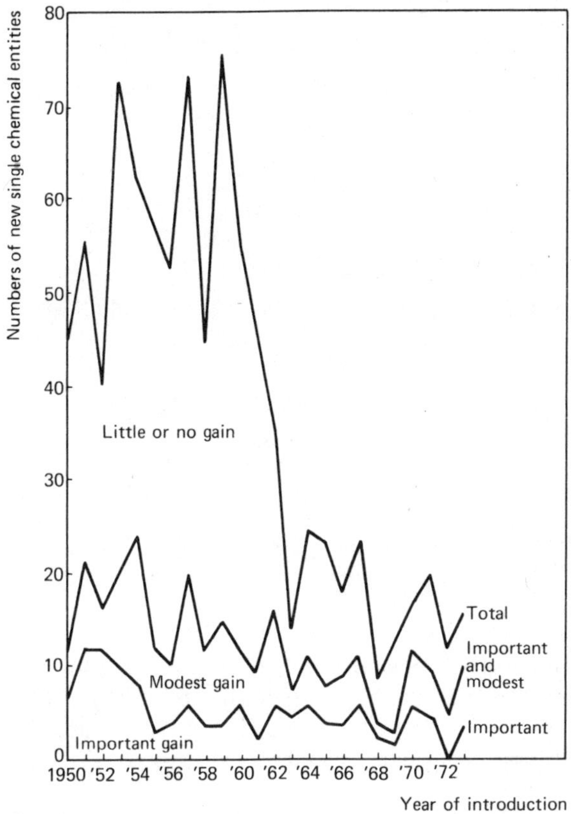

Fig. 7.2. FDA classification of annual new drug approvals by degree of therapeutic importance (1950–73).
Source: Grabowski, *op. cit.*, p. 22.

restricted to FDA defined uses. This results in a loss of consumer welfare equal to the area *GHDA*. It was this area which Peltzman measured. Conversely, if the Amendments provided benefits to consumers then it could be due to a reduction in the number of ineffective of NCEs launched. Peltzman argues that if ineffective drugs are marketed then demand for them will be initially and artificially inflated due to promotional claims. Such inflated demand will not persist as patients and physicians gain experience and the demand curves will shift down to the left. If *ADM* was an inflated demand curve, and *GHEN* the after-learning demand curve, then *HDE*

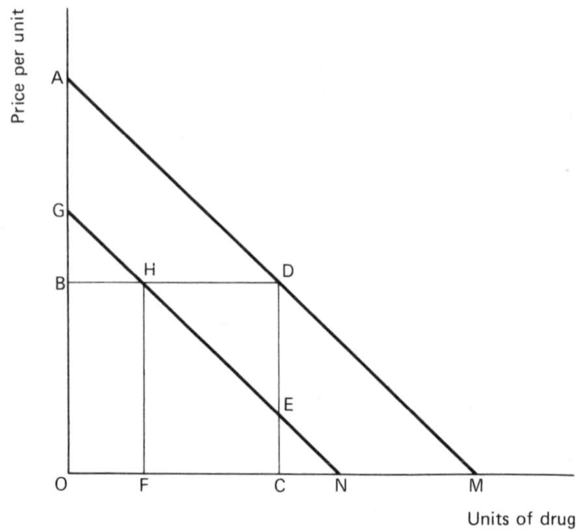

Fig. 7.3. Demand curves for new drugs.
Source: Peltzman, *op. cit.* (1974), p. 24.

represents the loss of consumer welfare due to mis-information in the pre-amendment situation. *HDE* would thus be eliminated by the 1962 Amendments. How long it would take *HDE* to be eliminated in the pre-amendment period would depend on the speed of the consumer learning process.

Peltzman calculated that an annual benefit loss (*GHDA*) of some $420 million annually was experienced by consumers as a result of the 1962 Amendments in the USA. If the $420 million was exaggerated by inaccurate perceptions of the true worth of pre-1962 NCEs then the difference between pre- and post-amendment new drug demand should narrow over time. Table 7.8 shows that even after a four-year learning period pre-1962 NCEs held or increased their market share (albeit with slight price reductions) while post-1962 NCEs performed almost as well. In short, the stability of market shares for pre-1962 drugs does not suggest that patients and doctors regarded their initial evaluations as exaggerated. At the very most Pelzman calculated that the removal of *HDE* reduced the $420 million loss to $330 million per annum.

Peltzman's work can be summarised by stating that the 1962 Amendments (1) cut the number of new drugs brought to the market each year by half with no corresponding reduction in inefficacious

Table 7.8. Weighted average market shares and relative prices for new drugs, one and four years after introduction

	Market share %		Relative price ratio	
	One year after launch	Four years after launch	One year after launch	Four years after launch
NCEs				
1960–62	8.3	8.3	1.4	1.3
1964–66	4.9	3.8	1.2	1.2
Other Drugs				
1960–62	6.4	7.7	1.1	1.1
1964–66	2.5	2.3	1.2	1.2

Source: Peltzman, *op. cit.* (1974), p. 37.

drugs (as defined by physicians and patients, not as defined by 'experts') and so imposed substantial net social costs from mortality and morbidity which could have been prevented if the development of new drugs had not been hampered by the Amendments. Peltzman's results, and the fact that R & D costs had increased substantially more in the USA than elsewhere, might well have been ignored had they not received confirmation from work done in the University of Rochester's Medical School. Dr Rita Ricardo Campbell points out that 'Peltzman could not name any drug which had not been approved in the United States, and which his analysis showed should have been approved' when asked to do so at a Senate Sub-Committee in 1973.[18] His study had employed aggregates and his inability to be specific damaged his credibility.

Wardell and Lasagna,[14] of Rochester, however, filled this gap in the knowledge. They found that from 1962 to 1971 nearly four times as many new drugs became available in the UK as in the USA; that for drugs marketed in both countries twice as many were introduced first in Britain as in the USA; that specialist physicians in the USA were often unaware of the drug lag but when informed of the existence of new effective drugs abroad wished they were available in America; that Britain exercised a more permissive policy towards new drugs but a stricter post-marketing surveillance of innovations. Wardell and Lasagna thus recommended an intensification of surveillance of new drugs *after* launch in the USA.

These studies in combination have changed official American attitudes to the stringent regulation pervasive on that side of the

Atlantic. In 1972 Dr Henry Simmons, then Director of the FDA's Bureau of Drugs argued that 'a drug lag in market availability of new effective drugs in the United States *vis-à-vis* other countries did not exist'.[19] Two years later, his successor, Dr Crout, stated, 'the data cited by Dr Wardell are correct. There were no approvals in hypertensive drugs in the first decade after the amendents. There were no approvals in the cardiovascular area in the years between 1967 and 1972, and that is . . . one of the causes of . . . the drug lag business'.[20] Commissioner Schmidt, a month later, stressed that the lag could only 'be remedied by Congressional and public recognition that the *failure* (italics in original) to approve an important new drug can be as detrimental to the public health as the approval of a potentially bad drug'.[21]

As the USA moves from negative to positive controls is the UK consolidating on or improving its favourable legislative climate? Regulation of innovation in Britain is primarily controlled by the Committee on Safety of Drugs (CSD) which was renamed the Committee on Safety of Medicines (CSM) after the passing of the 1968 Medicines Act. The CSD was a small, quasi-independent flexible organisation. With the Act, the operating methods of the Committee have been incorporated into law. 'Registration procedures have become mandatory. They are no longer voluntary. These changes are more than nominal. There is now a much more formal organisational structure and its character is veering towards that of the FDA. This is beginning to show in terms of the numbers employed and in concern at the speed of response to submissions'.[12]

Moreover the Chairman of the CSM. Sir Eric Scowen, now appears both to be doubting the ability of the physician and to be calling for stricter controls on the availability of new medicines. At a conference held at the Royal College of Physicians in late 1976 he said, 'if new substances were first prescribed for a limited number of people under surveillance, a better informed clinical judgement could be made at the time of the product's general introduction . . . It is now debatable whether all practitioners are equally competent to handle every new potent substance immediately after its introduction.'

In short, although decisions have yet to be taken, it may be that those responsible for the structure of controls in Britain have not learned from the American experience; that the British industry will move into a period of stultifying regulation just as its American counterpart emerges from a costly legislative straitjacket. In the final analysis the safety of a drug depends not on a Committee but on the prescriber and his decision, given the relevant clinical and psychological circumstances of his patient. Dr Lasagna, writing in *Medical Tribune* in 1962, put this point briefly but effectively when he said, 'on the basis of the best available information, Marilyn Monroe would be alive today if she had been given thalidomide instead of barbiturates for sedation. This fact is one which illustrates difficulties in dealing glibly with the advantages and disadvantages of useful drugs'.

8 Politics and Profits

BACKGROUND AND TREND

Before examining this general issue, we wish to direct attention to the distribution of rates of return between leading companies in the industry, since this analysis provides an indicator of the underlying market factors. It also affects the validity of some of the arguments advanced against high profits in the industry. Table 8.1 indicates the widely differing profit-levels of companies selling more than £1 million of medicines to the NHS. The first lesson is that whatever the benefits attributed to monopolistic elements in the market (patents, brand names, advertising, innovation), they are clearly not equally shared by all companies. The notion that high profits automatically accrue from having the sick as 'captive customers' and taking out a patent does not

Table 8.1. Distribution of profit levels: large companies return on capital; home sales of NHS medicines

	Per cent of total companies in each profit range					
	Rate of return %	1963–65 %	1969 %		1972 %	
Losses:			6		14.5	
Profit:	0–5	6	10	19	7	28.5
	5–10		3		7	
	10–15	13	10		19	
	15–20	6	26		19	
	20–25	38	13		14	
	25–30	6	13		10	
	Over 30	31	19		9.5	
		100	100		100	

Source: Sainsbury, *op. cit.*, p. 110, and DHSS returns. Reprinted in *Competition, Risk and Profit in the Pharmaceutical Industry* (Runnymede Research), p. 10.

1963–65. Three companies were discovered to be earning at between 50 and 55 per cent profit, some 30 per cent more than the modal group of companies at 20–25 per cent.

Curiously, the Report made no mention whatever of the record of these three companies in periods prior to 1963. One was the Beecham Group. This company, however, ran its pharmaceutical operations at a loss for the preceding sixteen years while the massive and world-renowned research effort of Professor Chain and his colleagues was being financed in Rome and in the Beecham Laboratories in England. This resulted in the isolation of the penicillin nucleus and in the stream of new semi-synthetic penicillin variants that is still emanating from this company. A 50 per cent profit in any one period is not in itself either reasonable or unreasonable. It must be looked at in the context of the activities of the company over time.

One of the main criticisms of the Sainsbury Report is that it never mentioned what the *average* rate of return on capital in the industry was. Only a range (Table 8.1) was examined and that was compared with the UK industrial average. Yet the VPRS, according to the Monopolies Commission Report on Librium and Valium, provided for 'negotiations about the reasonableness of profits . . . having regard to . . . the profitability of UK manufacturing industry as a whole'.[5] This point was taken up by Dr. Anthony Henfrey[6] who argued that individual pharmaceutical firms should not be compared with the general run of industries. But rather, pharmaceutical profits *on average* should only be compared with industries exhibiting the *same* general characteristics.

Most comentators err in relying on a single financial ratio for assessing profitability without regard to features peculiar to the accounting conventions of the firm or industry studied. There are several significant measures for return on capital alone. Two such yardsticks are displayed in Table 8.2 (respectively pre-tax profits and equity earnings as percentages of net tangible assets). High pre-tax profits are not unique to drugs but apply also to industries with high levels of intangible assets, such as advertising agencies (goodwill) or electronics and office equipment (R & D expenditure), or television rental companies who have low book values for their tangible assets due to policies of rapidly writing off, for depreciation purposes, the equipment they rent to their customers.

What these industries have in common is that most of them also appear at the upper end of the range when different sectors of UK industry are ranked by order of growth rates of assets and earnings over stand. In 1972 14.5 per cent of firms showed a loss, while 9.5 per ce showed a return on capital of over 30 per cent.

In the USA Conrad and Plotkin[1], and in UK Merrett and Cyria have shown that this wide variation is much more marked in pharm ceuticals than in industry generally. Their studies suggest that dru characterised by extreme riskiness in the form of a substant probability of either a negative return on investment or a very hi reward for success. Critics tend to focus on the upper extremes, with taking account of the fact that the prospect of a very high ret provides the inducement to invest in drugs, despite the larger risk losses. Moreover, Table 8.1 shows how, since 1963–65, the risk of a l or low return has substantially risen, whilst the prospect of exceptio success has sharply diminished. The 6 per cent of firms making a los a return below 10 per cent on capital had increased to 28.5 per cen 1972. Conversely, the 31 per cent of extremely successful firms mak over 30 per cent return on capital in 1963–65 had fallen to 9.5 per by 1972. In addition the most common rate of return in 1963–65, 2C per cent, fell to 15–20 per cent in 1969 and to 10–20 per cent in 19

Two main questions are raised by profitability figures. First, are fair and reasonable? Second, to what extent does the conti performance of R & D depend on profitability? The two are cl related. The Sainsbury Report spelt out the problem.

> There would be little inducement for firms to take on a specially risk in searching for a particular medicine which may be ea desired in medical practice if there were to be no possibili unusual profit and a high probability of failure after conside costs have been incurred. In such circumstances a 'normal' retu the sum risked would provide little inducement for a firm with alternative uses for its money to undertake research with high . . . We think . . . that in the absence of the prospect of 'abno profits, private industry would have no special inducem undertake research to which attached an abnormal risk of fa

After making this point the Report went on to conclude that profit levels in the industry were 'in some cases much higher than considered reasonable'.[4] It is hard to discover a rationale f conclusion, given that no attempt was made in the Report ei assess 'risk', or to relate drug profitability with returns on ca comparable industries. The conclusion was based on a study return on capital employed by pharmaceutical firms over the

Table 8.2. Profitability (1974) and Earnings (1974) in different sectors of British industry

Pretax profits as % net tangible assets*		**Equity earnings as % of net tangible assets**	
Advertising	54.3	Advertising	25.7
Oil	42.4	Oil	21.4
Pharmaceuticals	**34.6**	**Pharmaceuticals**	**18.6**
Office Equipment	32.3	Electronics	16.8
Electronics	32.2	Office Equipment	16.2
Radio & TV Rental	31.0	Radio & TV Rental	15.9
Domestic Appliances	30.5	Clothing	14.8
Clothing	28.3	Chemicals	14.0
Construction	27.1	Construction	13.3
Chemicals	25.7	Domestic Appliances	13.1
Aircraft	24.0	Food Manufacturing	12.6
Tobacco	23.1	Aircraft	12.2
Food Manufacturing	22.9	Heavy Electrical	11.5
Heavy Electrical	22.0	Tobacco	11.3
General Engineering	21.6	Shipping	11.2
Cement	21.5	Paper	10.8
Paper	21.2	Cement	10.7
Breweries	21.0	Breweries	10.5
Food Retailing	20.2	Food Retailing	10.4
Steel & Chemical Plant	18.9	Steel & Chemical Plant	9.8
Shipping	14.1	General Engineering	9.7
Department Stores	13.7	Department Stores	7.1
Hotels & Catering	13.0	Machine Tools	7.1
Machine Tools	12.9	Hotels & Catering	6.2

Based on latest published accounts of quoted UK companies: August 1974.

*Net tangible assets, land and buildings, plant and machinery, equipment and other fixed assets including goodwill, less depreciation, plus current assets, less current and deferred liabilities, less prior capital charges and minority interests. It therefore represents equity capital plus reserves.

Source: Runnymede Research, *op. cit.*, pp. 44–5.

the last ten years. Conversely, many of the apparently capital intensive sectors of industry such as shipping, machine tools, steel and chemical plant, appear distinctly unprofitable on this criterion of profitability and also appear at the lower end of rankings based on growth rates. In Henfrey's view the data show (contrast Tables 8.2 and 8.3) that the nearer the analysis approaches industrial growth rates, the less exceptional the return of pharmaceuticals becomes. At 14.5 per cent the growth rate of pharmaceutical earnings per share is 2.5 per cent above the industrial average of 11.9 per cent, whilst tangible assets have grown at 3 per cent per annum (10.2–7.2 per cent) faster than the market average (Table 8.3). 'Thus, by the standards of other *growth* (emphasis in original) industries, the ratio of pre-tax profits to net tangible assets of the pharmaceutical industry does not look excessive'.[7]

Table 8.3. Growth rates in different sectors of British industry (1965–74)

	Earnings* % p.a.		Assets† % p.a.
Total market	11.9		7.2
Oil	23.9	Contracting	15.1
Office Equipment	19.2	Hotels & Catering	14.5
Advertising	18.5	Office Equipment	14.0
Food Manufacturing	14.8	Advertising	11.3
Pharmaceuticals	**14.5**	Electrical Plant	10.4
Contracting	14.1	Food Retailing	10.4
Aircraft	13.9	**Pharmaceuticals**	**10.2**
Electronics	13.6	Tobacco	10.1
Hotels & Catering	12.5	Domestic Appliances	9.8
Food Retailing	12.2	Department Stores	9.7
Domestic Appliances	12.0	Clothing	9.3
Radio & TV Rental	11.4	Oil	8.2
Electrical Plant	11.3	Electronics	8.1
Chemicals	10.9	Food Manufacturing	7.8
Clothing	9.9	Breweries	6.8
Breweries	9.7	Cement	6.6
Tobacco	9.1	Aircraft	6.4
Cement	8.0	Radio & TV Rentals	5.8
Steel & Chemical Plant	7.7	General Engineering	5.3
Department Stores	7.6	Chemicals	4.9
Paper	4.9	Steel & Chemical Plant	4.7
General Engineering	4.0	Machine Tools	1.7
Machine Tools	0.4	Paper	1.5

*Average annual growth of earnings per share adjusted for capital changes.

†Average annual growth of net tangible assets per share adjusted for capital changes.
Based on latest published accounts of UK quoted companies.

Source: *ibid*., p. 47.

The implicit conclusions of the Merrett–Cyriax,[2] and the Conrad and Plotkin[1] studies of the 1960s, and Henfrey's investigation of the 1970s are that any apparently high level of profitability in the drug industry is due not to its monopolistic conduct but to the need to award a premium for risk, or to provide a premium to attract relatively more funds to finance relatively rapid growth. None of this is at odds with evidence examined in Chapters 4 and 5 on drug-industry pricing patterns.

CASH FLOW ANALYSIS

Another measure of profitability is provided by net cash flow (retained profits plus depreciation) as a percentage of sales (Table 8.4) since this goes some way towards adjusting profitability for the differing asset requirements of sectors of industry. Taking the 'growth' sectors, both radio and television rental companies and office-equipment manufacturers come out high on this method of assessing profitability since they incur heavy depreciation charges before arriving at profits. Drug firms come well down this list for the simple reason that they *apparently* have a small asset base, since their major asset, R & D expenditure, is written off against profits as it is incurred. Advertising and employment agencies come even further down on this ranking since they are basically goodwill operations with low levels of fixed assets.

In short, profits are no more than 'a conventional financial management symbol which is capable of definition and computation in a variety of ways'.[8] The subjectivity that is present in conventionally measured profit is mainly due to three accounting policy variables: depreciation, capitalisation and stock valuation. Only the first two concern us here. Depreciation charges depend on subjective estimates of asset life. Moreover, accountants cannot agree on whether or not to link the charges to historic, current or replacement costs. Capitalisation policy is concerned with deciding whether an expenditure is expected to produce benefits in successive accounting periods or whether benefits should be expected only in the period in which the expenditure is incurred. The former is generally capitalised, the latter is not.

IS R & D AN ASSET?

R & D should be regarded as an investment expenditure since it is incurred today with a view to generating benefits tomorrow. In

Table 8.4. Net cash flow as percentage of sales – selected British industries (1974)

Radio & TV Rental	24.8
Shipping	12.5
Oil	12.2
Electronics	10.8
Chemicals	10.3
Office Equipment	8.9
Cement	8.9
Domestic Appliances	6.9
Pharmaceuticals	**6.9**
Aircraft	5.7
Breweries	5.4
Heavy Electrical	5.3
Clothing	4.7
Construction	4.6
Paper	4.4
General Engineering	4.3
Advertising	4.3
Hotels & Catering	4.0
Tobacco	3.6
Food Manufacturing	3.5
Steel & Chemical Plant	2.9
Department Stores	2.9
Machine Tools	2.7
Food Retailing	2.2

Source: ibid., p. 44.

consequence R & D, like expenditure on plant and machinery, should be capitalised and carried as a balance-sheet item and subsequently written off as a cost of sales of the product developed by the research over the period in which the financial benefits arise. In fact the British Monopolies Commission has accepted 'that there is a practical case, on grounds of normal commercial prudence, and perhaps also of encouraging innovation for charging research expenditure against sales'.[9]

If R & D expenditures were capitalised in a firm's books the impact on its accounting rate of return would be twofold. First, the denominator, the capital employed, would be increased, this would have the effect of reducing the declared return on capital. Second, the numerator, the profits, would be altered. Whether profits would be increased or decreased would depend on the relative sizes of the depreciation charge levied against the R & D asset and the R & D expenditures which under traditional circumstances would be charged against profits as they occurred. Thus the numerator would be altered but whether up or down is unpredictable.

Capitalisation of R & D is realistic in economic terms. It may well produce adjusted rates of return reflecting profitability more accurately than conventional accounting procedures. But it is arguable, despite the Monopolies Commission's comment, that it would be 'imprudent'. First, R & D expenditure may turn out to be worthless, *ex post*. Second, the realisable value of the asset would be open to subjective interpretation. Third, cash flows (*i.e.* stated profits plus depreciation charges) could be boosted by amounts equivalent to the moneys spent on R & D during the accounting period but from which benefits had still (conditionally) to be derived.[10] These views, moreover, reflect those of the Institute of Chartered Accountants which in its Exposure Draft 14 recommends a Proposed Standard Accounting Practice in which expenditure on R & D is written off in the year in which it occurs.[11] In addition, of course, such write-offs minimise a firm's tax liability so the probability of published accounts capitalising R & D expenditure in the future is slight.

EMPIRICAL EVIDENCE

A major difficulty facing researchers in this field is to ascertain how much of a given year's R & D expenditures should be attributed to any one product. Then the question is begged as to how long an effective life the asset so created will have. In practice empirical adjustments to published accounts have all, *faute de mieux*, been worked at a highly aggregated level.

In 1969 Clymer[12] estimated that the *average* length of time between R & D expenditure and successful product launch was five years, followed by a further two years of heavy advertising expenditures before peak sales were achieved, and thirteen subsequent years of declining sales before market exit. Thus to the extent that Clymer's figures are correct (and have not changed as market circumstances have altered) one scenario might be to charge zero depreciation for seven years followed by one-thirteenth of the R & D (and promotional outlays) for the remaining period.

More or less sophisticated variants of Clymer's approach have been developed. Baily[13] argued that the main contribution of a product to

Table 8.5. The effect of capitalisation of R & D expenditures on return on capital (1969)

		Adjusted by the depreciation policy of:		
Reported return	%	Clymer	Baily	Bloch
Schering	44.0	27.8	29.2	32.1
SK and F	49.0	25.9	27.2	30.0
Parke Davis	15.6	11.9	12.1	12.7
Upjohn	29.2	19.1	19.9	21.6

Source: H. Bloch 'True Profitability Measures for Pharmaceutical Firms,' in Cooper (ed), *op. cit.*, p. 154.

profits comes in the year of launch. Thus in his study he suggests no depreciation charge for the first five years followed by a 15 per cent reducing balance charge for the totality of a product's market life. Block[14] argued for a policy that allowed a depreciation write-off in proportion to the sales of the product in any given year of its life. This argument was based on the thesis that R & D generates profits each year in proportion to the amount of sales arising from products emerging from the R & D effort.

Table 8.5 shows the impact on the 1969 rate of return for four major drug firms using the various depreciation policies on R & D expenditure suggested by Clymer, Baily and Bloch respectively. No matter which policy is adopted, the reported rate of return is considerably decreased.

These exercises, however, failed to incorporate all of the factors that create biases in the accounting rate of return (*e.g.* advertising expenditures, inflation adjustments, risk differences). Two more recent investigations by Ayanian[13] and Stauffer[14] capitalised both R & D and promotion expenditures to correct for biases in the accounting rate of return measures. Stauffer's study investigates one firm and Ayanian's examines six firms. There are other differences in the adjustments made in each. For example, Ayanian shows the effects of different depreciation rates for intangible capital expenditures ranging from 9 to 13 per cent. Stauffer uses varying depreciation techniques including declining exponential and straight-line depreciation. Again, as in Table 8.5, the corrected rates of return fell. While each of these five studies uses different methods for correcting rates of return and alternative data sources, the results they obtain all point in the same direction:

accounting rates of return in firms with intangible capital are biased upward.

Unfortunately all of these studies are based on small samples and are limited to pharmaceutical firms. They all fail to contrast their results with comparable corrections to profits in other industries. Kenneth Clarkson[15] in a recently published paper incorporated corrections for inflation, provided for the accumulation of capital during the basic research and development stages, and employed differing economic life-cycles for advertising, for basic research and for development, which vary among industries. His research also examined alternative opportunity costs of capital and averaged the results for periods longer than the typical business cycle. These corrections were applied to sixty-nine firms representing eleven industries with differing levels of intangible capital.

Clarkson argues that it would be highly unlikely that observed rates of return among firms within an industry or for all industries would be equal. Nevertheless, if biases from any one of these factors can be reduced, rates of return will move closer together if markets are competitive. If these biases have been reduced and markets are competitive, one would expect a narrowing of calculated rates of return.

Industry average accounting rates of return for 1959–73 were computed for each of the eleven industries and these are shown in Table 8.6. The corrected average rate of return significantly decreased for those industries which were relatively capital-intensive in promotion and R & D expenditures. The pharmaceutical and electrical industries, which spend relatively highly on these activities, experienced the largest changes in their 1959–73 average rates of return. (Clarkson argues that his results are extremely 'robust', and that the outcome would be little altered if any changes were made in his computational assumptions.)

The pharmaceutical industry experienced the largest decline in its rate of return. Its average corrected rate of return is 5.4 percentage points less than its average accounting return. The next largest drop in the electrical machinery industry is 3.2 percentage points. In the other nine industries, the return declines only about one percentage point. Overall, the estimated average rate of return in all industries falls from 11.2 to 9.6 per cent. More important, the variance, when corrections have been made, falls substantially from 7.5 to 2.5.

Despite a 5.4 per cent fall, drug-industry profits remain the highest, as they are prior to correction. It would be surprising if differences did not persist, however. First, neither the crude nor the correct rates at any

Table 8.6. Average accounting and corrected rates of return on net worth (1959–73) (percentages for selected American industries)

Industry	Accounting rates of return	Corrected rates of return	Difference
Pharmaceuticals	18.3	12.9	–5.4
Electrical machinery	13.3	10.1	–3.2
Foods	11.8	10.6	–1.2
Petroleum	11.2	10.8	–0.4
Chemicals	10.6	9.1	–1.5
Paper	10.5	10.1	–0.4
Office machinery	10.5	9.9	–0.6
Motor vehicles	10.5	9.2	–1.3
Rubber products	10.1	8.7	–1.4
Aerospace	9.2	7.4	–1.8
Ferrous metals	7.6	7.3	–0.3
Average	11.2	9.6	–1.6
Variance	7.5	2.5	

Source: K. Clarkson, *Intangible Capital and Rates of Return* (Washington, D.C.: American Enterprise Institute, 1977), p. 64.

time need reflect steady-state returns because industries are rarely in equilibrium for long periods. Second, there are differences in riskiness among different industries, with higher average rates of return required for competitive viability in riskier industries. Some industries, like pharmaceuticals,[1,2] are extremely risky; only some firms gain high returns. Third, entry barriers such as those erected by government regulations could cause observed rates of return in some industries to be higher than in others.[16] This last point may well have affected the profits of *existing* large drug firms since the 1962 Amendments. We have already seen how these appear to favour the large performer of R & D at the expense of the smaller.

PROFITS : A DECLINING INCENTIVE?

Drug-industry profits are high but variable. When corrected to their 'true' economic level they remain high relative to many other industries. In Britain the historic trend is downwards. Schwartzman[17] estimates that in the USA drug firms in 1973 were earning only 3.3 per cent after taxes on their R & D expenditure. This contrasts with an almost 12 per cent after tax return in the early 1960s.

To calculate an expected rate of return on the total costs of developing the new drugs that were introduced between 1966 and 1972 Schwartzman estimates the R & D expenditures that went into producing them and the current and future profits that they will generate. Assuming a 30 per cent pre-tax profit margin and a 15-year commercial life, he estimates a net profit of $1.4 million per year for each drug. He puts the average cost of discovery and development at $24.4 million, or $12.2 million after taxes, which is spread over a 10-year estimated development period. This works out to an expected after-tax rate of return of 3.3 per cent on R & D investment.

Even when he uses a higher gross profit margin and a longer commercial life, Schwartzman's computations produce rates of return that are still surprisingly low. At a 40 per cent margin and 20-year life, for example, he estimates only a 7.5 per cent rate of return. Based on the same assumptions, this compares with an 18.4 per cent rate in 1960, when the average cost of R & D for an approved drug was only $1.3 million. Schwartzman's results, of course, beg the question as to why firms continue to invest in drug R & D when they could (apparently) earn more elsewhere. One explanation is simply that Schwartzman's calculations correctly indicate a trend but depend on historical data to predict an outcome much more pessimistic than will in fact occur. Firms' R & D procedures will have adapted to the new requirements of the 1960s and 1970s; and the old gross margins may no longer be applicable in calculating expected rates of return. (This explantion fits in with the data of Tables 4.2 and 4.3 in Chapter 4.)

Schwartzman,[18] however, does not find the behaviour of the drug companies all that baffling. Some companies think that they can do better than the industry average. Others have already invested huge sums in R & D and cannot economically discontinue their research activities. Still others are banking on a major breakthrough that may lead to a host of new innovations. Schwartzman insists that these expectations will only last in the short run. In the long run, the low rate of return spells, if not an absolute decline in R & D spending, then clearly a continued reduction in the number of research projects that companies undertake.

9 Conclusions

The main conclusions of this study can be set down in a series of findings:

1. The drug industry is a young, research intensive industry.
2. It has made immense contributions to the health and well-being of people in all countries.
3. Large areas of disease remain which probably can be conquered with further pharmacological advances.
4. Contrary to drug-industry expectations the value of ethical pharmaceutical sales have continued a strong upward trend. During 1968–76 growth took place at an average annual compound rate of 13.5 per cent per year, and the world market in 1976 was valued at over $40,000 million. Based on historical growth rates the world market could more than double by 1982 to over $90,000 million. This growth could be achieved providing:

   i. Expectations of health and intolerance of illness continue to rise into the 1980s.
   ii. The industry continues its past policies of marketing specialities which are patentable, highly innovative and which have world markets, and for which premium prices, designed to recoup R & D expenses, can be charged.
   iii. That the expansion of the market, due mainly to growth in the developed markets, will not be seriously impeded by a deterioration in the regulatory climate making introductory and maintenance marketing more difficult and expensive.

5. Growth in the Third World countries is both marginal and unsure. Whilst the multi-nationals are aware of their social responsibilities towards the developing world, the drive towards indigenisation in the drug industry in those countries will inevitably conflict with the local operations of the international drug companies. If health-care standards are to be enhanced in the Third World countries they cannot afford to alienate the multi-nationals. Primary problem

areas are:

i. The threat of indigenisation at best and nationalisation at worst will not encourage the multi-nationals to establish subsidiaries or to expand their present facilities in the developing countries. Progress towards self-sufficiency in drugs should be gradual and carried out by the Third World in co-operation with the industry rather than by placing itself in a position of conflict.

ii. The efforts of WHO in producing a short list of essential drugs for Third World countries is a short-term expediency designed quickly to extend an improved level of health care to a wider population — and should not be seen as a recipe for the creation of an indigenous industry. The key to development in this area is to co-operate with those commercial organisations in each country, and for the industry to be allowed to produce and distribute the drugs on the list — together with the other specialities produced by each company.

iii. Irrespective of production and marketing considerations the countries of the Third World must consider the implications of restricting commercial pharmaceutical company operations. Only these companies have the unique R & D capabilities to surmount the special medical and therapy problems of the Third World countries. R & D programmes are being directed by the major companies towards the discovery of Third World specific drugs. To cut the commercial companies off from their markets would necessarily bring such programmes to a halt.

6. The regulatory climate in which the industry operates is becoming increasingly stringent, and the atmosphere of trust between public, industry and government, is being eroded. To a great extent the blame for this must be ascribed to the politicians, whose emotive and public posturing on industry profits has attracted greater publicity than the industry's rather low-key refutations. Unfortunately it is not the politicians who suffer from the consequences of such action, but the public at large, as in such an atmostphere the drug companies are loosing interest in carrying out basic research and are turning increasingly to defensive development and marketing, which is reducing the numbers of innovatory drugs entering the market.
7. As far as cost savings are concerned the more direct means emphasised by governments and health insurance funds have failed

to make a significant impact. The stringency of entry regulations and such costs are passed inevitably to the consumer or whoever funds the health-care system. Government ambivalence in the pricing/research question has led companies to:

i. Move into less-regulated industrial fields where profits are high and R & D expenses are low.
ii. Move out of the high-risk/high-cost area of basic research into the development of 'me too' drugs.
iii. Move into the area of R & D by 'molecular roulette', concentrating on developing new forms of existing therapy with marginal advantages.

8. Since drugs do not fall within the category of expenditures on unforeseen and large catastrophes (they are absolutely inexpensive and are also cheap relative to personal incomes : illness is not a rare occurrence) it is at least arguable that drugs should not be paid for on the insurance principle (private or state); this would encourage a more responsible attitude to their consumption, and conceivably also towards the consumption of other health-care and social-welfare provisions.
9. The industry is 'competitive' by almost all yardsticks used by economists:

i. Entry is frequent and easy.
ii. Prices tend to be forced towards marginal cost.
iii. Promotion facilitates entry and innovation.
iv. Profitability is not dissimilar to that experienced by comparable industries.
v. Scale economies are unimportant.

10. Government regulatory activity, however, has been founded on the belief that the industry is not competitive and has:

i. Imposed price restraints.
ii. Effected profit controls.
iii. Laid down promotional constraints.
iv. Increased or introduced safely and efficacy guidelines.

11. These regulatory activities have:

   i. Strengthened the generic sector of the industry which could well become 'perfectly competitive' but which by definition is non-innovative and makes no pretence to be so.
   ii. Raised entry barriers to the innovative sector of the industry by: (*a*) Restricting the promotion which facilitates entry; and (*b*) imposing regulations which have made R & D susceptible to scale economies and an activity which only large firms can perform.
   iii. Reduced the attractiveness of entry by: (*a*) Imposing downward pressure on prices and profits; and (*b*) exerting upward pressure on costs.
   iv. By dint of (ii) and (iii) the innovative sector of the industry may be becoming less competitive.
   v. Removed pharmacological benefits from consumers, either in the future as a consequence of reducing the attractiveness of current R & D, or in the present (as in the USA) by over-zealously protecting the public from drug hazards but not from disease.

In a recent paper[1] Michael Cooper concludes:

> In the long-run, however, prospects can only be good. No government is willingly going to risk depriving its citizens of access to the latest therapeutic advance ... New growth points (diagnostic aids, memory drugs and so on), falling sickness thresholds and changes in environment and life-style will all ensure the continuation of a rapidly expanding market

We agree with his analysis of demand. We wish we could share his optimism about the impact of government on supply. But until politicians are judged by the yardstick of forgone alternatives we fear a continuance of their myopic behaviour.

Notes

NOTES TO CHAPTER 1

1. G. E. Trease, *Pharmacy in History* (London, 1964), p. 235.
2. R. Calder, *The Lifer Savers* (Pan, 1961), p. 20.
3. For a fuller and more informative discussion on the story behind modern pharmaceuticals, L. G. Matthews, *A History of Pharmacy in Britain* (Edinburgh 1962), is recommended.
4. H. M. Bottcher, *Miracle Drugs* (Heinemann, 1959), p. 190.
5. The remainder of this paragraph relies heavily on Michael H. Cooper, *Substitute Competition, Government Regulation and the International Pharmaceutical Industry*, University of Otago, Economics Discussion Papers, No. 7701, 1977.
6. Paul de Haen, Inc., New York.
7. *Gaps in Technology — Pharmaceuticals*, OECD, 1969, p. 23.
8. Jerome Schnee, 'Innovation and Discovery in the Drug Industry' in *Research and Innovation in the Modern Corporation*, E. Mansfield *et al.* (eds) (Macmillan, 1971) p. 174.
9. Cited in Michael H. Cooper, *Prices and Profits in the Pharmaceutical Industry* (Pergamon, 1966) pp. 116–117.
10. W. S. Comanor, 'The Drug Industry and Medical Research: The Economics of the Kefauver Committee Investigation', *Journal of Business*, 1966.
11. J. Y. Bogue, 'Organisation and Economics of Research in the Pharmaceutical Industry', *Pharmaceutical Journal*, 1962.
12. J. T. Litchfield, 'Evaluation of Drugs in Experimental Animals' P. Talalay (ed.), *Drugs in Our Society* (Johns Hopkins, 1960).
13. D. Schwartzman, *The Expected Return from Pharmaceutical Research* (American Enterprise Institute, 1975).
14. B. A. Weisbrod, *Economics of Public Health* (University of Pennsylvania Press, 1961) pp. 30–1.
15. Department of Health and Social Security, *Annual Reports*, 1957, 1967 and 1975.
16. S. Taylor, *Good General Practice* (1954).
17. A. I. Harris, E. Cox, C. R. W. Smith, *Handicapped and Impaired in Britain* (HMSO, 1971).

NOTES TO CHAPTER 4

1. For example many countries have price regulation or control schemes. Others have rules which discourage or prohibit prescribers from choosing drugs which are priced above a given level. An example of the former is

Britain's Pharmaceutical Price Regulation Scheme (PPRS) and an example of the latter is the Maximum Allowable Cost (MAC) regulation in the USA. In general MAC sets limits on the amount the Department of Health, Education and Welfare (HEW) will reimburse for drugs having multiple sources of supply.

2. The Beveridge Report, *Social Insurance and Allied Services* HMSO, 1942) was the progenitor of the NHS. In it the assumption was made that a health care scheme, free at the point of consumption, would cost the Exchequer £130 million per annum. The Report argued that the figure would be little different 20 years after the establishment of the NHS itself. In the event, the NHS Bill of 1946 estimated the annual cost at £110 million, but after the first eight months of operation the cost of the NHS was already running at an annual rate of twice that figure. The foundation for these forecasting errors was the belief that free health care provision would, by improving the overall health of the population proved to be a self-eliminating expense. But the impact on demand of both a zero price and of changing attitudes to illness, and to supply of changing technologies of diagnosis and therapy, disproved this argument. For a fuller description of the legal background to the NHS and investigation of both it and the drug industry *see* F. H. Happold, *Medicine at Risk*, (Queen Anne Press, 1967) pp. 3–9. For reviews of changes in the demand for and supply of health care resources and their impact on the health care industry *see Prospects in Health* (Office of Health Economics, 1971) and *The Health Care Dilemma* (Office of Health Economics, 1975).
3. *The Cost of the National Health Service in England and Wales* (HMSO, 1956) (Guillebaud Report).
4. *Final Report of the Committee on the Cost of Prescribing* (HMSO, 1959) (Hinchcliffe Report).
5. *Ibid.*, p. 27.
6. *Administered Prices: Drugs*. U.S. Senate Sub-Committee on Antitrust (1961) (Kefauver Report).
7. *Ibid.*, p. 34.
8. For example, Henry Steele, 'Patents, Restrictions and Price Competition in the Ethical Drug Industry', *Journal of Industrial Economics* (1964). Brian Inglis, *Drugs, Doctors and Disease* (Mayflower, 1962).
9. *Report of the Committee of Enquiry into the Relationship of the Pharmaceutical Industry with the National Health Service, 1965–1967* (Sainsbury Report, 1967).
10. Sainsbury argued that when drugs became multi-source, the products 'may (have) become widely known under names that are the private property of particular manufacturers because a large amount of money has been spent on advertising these (brand) names. Successful sales promotion may not infrequently permit a manufacturer to charge higher prices for his product even though it is identical with others on the market.' *Ibid.*, Para. 282.
11. *Ibid.*, p. 2.
12. *The British Patent System*, Cmnd. 4407 (HMSO, 1970) (Banks Committee Report).
13. In addition the Government can and has referred firms to the Monopolies and Restrictive Practices Commission. For example Roche's products

Librium and Valium was statutarily reduced in price as a consequence of the Monopolies Commission Report *Chlordiazepoxide and Diazepan*, HC, 197, 1973 (HMSO, 1973), Roche was condemned for charging prices for the two drugs which were 'manifestly too high'. The Commission did report that their daily dosage costs were 'amongst the lowest when compared with competitive products' but then went on to claim that there was a '*virtual absence of price competition*' (emphasis added).

14. Reported from a speech by Alan Beard, Controller of Supply, DHSS to the Pharmaceutical Manufacturers Association of the USA (*ABPI News*), September (1977)).
15. *Ibid.*
16. *Ibid.*
17. *Ibid.*
18. In 1970 the top five firms controlled 29.7 per cent of the international market. A further 50 or so firms were active participants. *Source: Proposed Beecham-Glaxo, Boots-Glaxo Mergers*, Monopolies Commission (HMSO, 1972), p. 66. The industry is even more diffusely structured in the national British market. Conversely, only 28 out of all 335 Product Groups in all UK industry had five firm concentration ratios of under 30 per cent in 1968. *Source: Report on the Census of Production*, 1968 (HMSO, 1974), pt. 158, table 44.
19. *See* John S. McGee, 'In Defence of Industrial Concentration', in Yale Brozen (ed) *The Competitive Economy* (General Learning Press, 1975), p. 40–2.
20. F. M. Scherer, *Industrial Structure and Economic Performance* (Read McNally, 1971) p. 17.
21. H. Steele, 'Monopoly and Competition in the Ethical Drugs Market', *Journal of Law and Economics* (1962).
22. W. S. Comanor, 'Research and Competitive Product Differentiation in the Pharmaceutical Industry in the United Sector, *Economica*, (1964).
23. Kefauver Report, *op. cit.*
24. Kefauver, *In a Few Hands* (Pelican, 1966) p. 34.
25. *Ibid.*, p. 29.
26. Comanor, *op. cit.*, p. 373.
27. *Ibid.*
28. *Ibid.*
29. Steele, *op. cit.*, p. 136.
30. Comanor, *op. cit.*, p. 375.
31. Steele, *op. cit.*, p. 161.
32. HC 197, *op. cit.*
33. Sainsbury, *op. cit.*
34. Cooper, MH 1967, *Prices and Profits in the Pharmaceutical Industry* (Oxford: Pergamon) p. 43.
35. J. K. Galbraith, *The New Industrial State* (Boston and New York: Houghton Mifflin; London: André Deutsch, 1967) p. 110.
36. Comanor, *op. cit.*, p. 372.
37. Cooper, *op. cit.*
38. Reekie, W. Duncan, *The Economics of the Pharmaceutical Industry*, (London: Macmillan, 1975) p. 37.

39. Monopolies Commission. *Parallel Pricing*. Cmnd. 5330 (London: HMSO, 1973).
40. Sainsbury, *op. cit.*, p. 16.
41. F. M. Scherer, *Industrial Pricing* (London and Chicago: Rand McNally, 1972) pp. 45–52.
42. Section 41. This Section allowed an applicant to obtain a licence as of right for any patent on foods and medicines *only*. It did not apply to other products. The discriminating provisions of Section 41 were not included in the new 1977 Patents Acts.
43. *Hansard*, November 1975.
44. *The Financial Times*, 7 April 1976.
45. *International Price Competions*, Chemicals EDC (HMSO, 1972).
46. For example Miltown, a leading early tranquiliser, has a recommended dosage range of 400–800 mgs., thrice daily. Librium is recommended on a 10 mgs., thrice daily regimen; and Nobrium, a recent tranquiliser, has a recommended regimen of 5 mgs., thrice daily. In antibiotics Penbritin's four by 250 mgs. regimen has been replaced by Talpen's three by 250 mgs. daily dosage. Terramycin, with a four by 250 mgs. regimen can now be replaced with Vibramycin's single 100 mgs. dose. Source: *Monthly Index of Medical Specialities* (1976).
47. G. Polanyi and P. Polanyi, *Competition, Risk and Profit in the Pharmaceutical Industry* (London: Runnymede Reasearch, 1975) pp. 31–2.
48. J. A. Schumpeter, *Capitalism, Socialism and Democracy* (Harrap, 1947) p. 105. Schumpeter noted that 'the bulk of what we call economic progress' is incompatible with perfect competition since neither the resources nor the incentive for innovation exist in these conditions.
49. J. F. Weston, *Pricing in the Pharmaceutical Industry* (Los Angeles: University of California, 1977).
50. *See above* p. 84
51. Weston, *op. cit.*
52. Mark A. Schankerman, *Common Costs in Pharmaceutical Research and Development: Implications for Direct Price Regulation*, in Samuel A. Mitchell and Emery A. Link (eds), *Impact of Public Policy on Drug Innovation and Pricing* (American University Press, 1976) pp. 3–45.
53. *Ibid.*, p. 12.
54. W. J. Baumol R. Bradford, 'Optimal Departures from Marginal Cost Pricing', *American Economic Review* (1970).
55. Milton Friedman, *Essays in Positive Economics* (Chicago, 1974) p. 21.
56. Douglas C. Cocks, 'Product Innovation and the Dynamic Elements of Competition in the Ethical Pharmaceutical Industry', in Robert B. Helms (ed) *Drug Development and Marketing* (American Enterprise Institute, 1975) pp. 225–54.
57. Eli W. Clemens, 'Price Discrimination and the Multiple Product Firm', *Review of Economic Studies*, XIX pp. 1–11 (1951).
58. Cocks, *op. cit.*
59. Doctors *do* tend to price-discriminate between patients according to their ability to pay. Thus marginal consumers to tend to be charged lower prices for not dissimilar services. Thus, *a priori*, a doctor may well provide a drug with a lower monetary price to a marginal patient even if higher-quality,

more efficacious, but higher-priced medicaments are also available. In other words the necessary price discrimination on which the main argument of the text depends is accomplished for the drug industry by the normal medical practice of the doctor. *See* R. A. Kessels, 'Price Discrimination in Medicine', *Journal of Law and Economics* (1958).

NOTES TO CHAPTER 5

1. Sanjaya Lall, 'The Pharmaceutical Industry and Less-Developed Countries, with Special Reference to India', *Bulletin of the Oxford Institute of Economics and Statistics* (1974).
2. Jesse W. Markham, 'Economic Incentives in the Drug Industry,' *Drugs in Our Society*, Paul Talalay, ed. (Baltimore: Johns Hopkins Press, 1964) p. 170.
3. Douglas L. Cocks and John R. Virts, 'Pricing Behavior of the Ethical Pharmaceutical Industry', *Journal of Business* (1974).
4. David Schwartzman, *Innovation in the Pharmaceutical Industry* (Johns Hopkins, 1977) p. 251.
5. *Ibid.*, p. 298.
6. Lester Telser, 'The Supply Response to Shifting Demand in the Ethical Pharmaceutical Industry', R. B. Helms (ed), *Drug Development and Marketing, op. cit.*
7. On the other hand the measure has the defect of ignoring successful net entry between 1963 and a departure date prior to 1972. This could be non-trivial criticism.
8. W. D. Reekie, 'Barriers to Entry and Competition', in G. Teeling-Smith (ed), *Economics and Innovation in the Pharmaceutical Industry* (Office of Health Economics, 1969) p. 3.
9. *Ibid.*, p. 2.
10. W. Duncan Reekie, *Pricing New Pharmaceutical Products* (Croom Helm, 1977).
11. NEDO, *Innovative Activity in the Pharmaceutical Industry* (National Economic Development Office, 1973).
12. Irrespective of which index is used, the results are virtually identical.
13. Joel Dean, *Managerial Economics* (Prentice-Hall, 1947).
14. Scherer, *Industrial Pricing, op. cit.*, p. 129.
15. Jules Dupuit, 'On the Measurement of the Utility of Public Works', in *Readings in Welfare Economics*, K. J. Arrow and T. Scitovsky (eds) (Allen and Unwin, 1969).
16. M. H. Cooper. *European Pharmaceutical Prices, 1964–1974*. (London: Croom Helm, 1975).
17. *See* Reuben A. Kessels, 'Price Discrimination in Medicine', *Journal of Law and Economics* (1958).
18. The table is restricted to the 171 NCEs for which FDA ratings were available.
19. This latter conclusion is statistically as well as economically significant. The Yates' Corrected Chi-squared for the table is 70.501. This is significant at

the 1 per cent level and would not be meaningfully altered by movement of the price boundaries or by finer subdivision of the price classifications. The contingency coefficient is 0.54 (while a 3 × 3 table has a maximum contingency value of 0.816).

20. Lall, *op. cit.* p. 149, suggests that in drugs there is 'a great deal of wasteful expenditure on imitative R & D and patenting ... research (is directed) primarily at the production of marketable rather than therapeutically new products'.
21. *See above*, p. 95–8.
22. *See above*, p. 99.
23. *See above*, pp. 100–1.
24. Sam Peltzman, *The Regulation of Pharmaceutical Innovation* (Washington: American Enterprise Institute, 1974) finds that slowing the rate of introduction of NCEs slows the rate at which the prices of old drugs fall. This suggests that the hedonic (or quality adjusted) prices of NCEs are set below those of old drugs and all producers of these drugs are forced to respond by meeting this price competition. The fact that old drug prices fell, most of which were on patent, means that patented drug prices respond to the prices of newly introduced drugs and, by inference, also respond to changes in prices for other patented drugs as well as to the prices of newly introduced drugs.
25. *See above*, p. 94.
26. Lall, *op. cit.*, p. 150.
27. G. J. Stigler, 'The Economics of Information', *Journal of Political Economy* (1962).
28. The fact that the drop in variance is statistically significant is shown by the F ratios.
29. *Ibid.*
30. A less charitable explanation might be that the NCE is a 'completely spurious differentiation' backed by heavy promotional expenditure to provide it with a 'strong monopolistic' position (Lall, *op. cit.*, p. 151) and that competitors treat it as a focal point for collusive price leadership. This argument collapses, however, since if 'the promotion and sale of ineffective drugs' (Lall, *op. cit.*, p. 153) is, in fact, possible at a premium price then why should such a premium not be maintained?
31. *The Drug Users* Background Paper, Department of Health, Education and Welfare, Task Force on Prescription Drugs (Washington: Government Printing Office, 1969) p. 16.
32. John M. Firestone, *Trends in Prescription Drug Prices*, AEI Special Analysis, (Washington: 1970).
33. John M. Firestone, *Prescription Size Index, 1975* (mimeographed) Pharmaceutical Manufacturers' Association (Washington).
34. John R. Virts, 'Economic Regulation of Prescription Drugs' (mimeographed) Paper presented to a Seminar on the Economics of the Pharmaceutical Industry, University of California, Los Angeles (1977).

NOTES TO CHAPTER 6

1. Sainsbury, *op. cit.*, p. 71.
2. *Ibid.*, p. 64.
3. Reported in *Sources of Information for Prescribing Doctors in Britain* (OHE, 1977) p. 16.
4. Max Adle, *Modern Market Research* (Crosby Lockwood, 1968) p. 112.
5. In addition the government agreed that Section 41, the compulsory licensing provision of the 1949 Patents Acts, which applies *only* to food and drugs, would be dropped in the 1977–78 revision of the Act. *ABPI News*, June (1977).
6. Department of Health, *Annual Report* (1972), p. 12.
7. ABPI, *Annual Report* (1967) p. 7.
8. *The Economist*, 5 July 1969, p. 20.
9. US House of Representatives, *Hearings before the Anti-trust and Monopoly Sub-Committee, 1961–62.*
10. Sainsbury, *op. cit.*, p. 102.
11. Cooper, *op. cit.*, p. 94.
12. PAC, *Minutes of Evidence* (1964–65) Class 6, Vote 8, Appendix V.
13. *British Medical Journal*, 30 March 1968.
14. A. W. Beckett, 'The Cost of Safety in Medicines', in G. Teeling-Smith (ed), *The Pharmaceutical Industry and Society* (OHE, 1972).
15. Sainsbury, *op. cit.*, p. 78.
16. R. Harris and Seldon, *Advertising and the Public* (Deutsch, 1962) p. 75.
17. R. Bauer and M. Field, 'Ironic Constrast: US and USSR Drug Industries', *Harvard Business Review* (1962).
18. Sam Peltzman, 'The Diffusion of Pharmaceutical Innovation' in Helms, *op. cit.*

NOTES TO CHAPTER 7

1. J. Schumpeter, *Capitalism, Socialism and Democracy* (Harrap, 1950).
2. The Monopolies Commission, *Beecham Group Ltd. and Glaxo Group Ltd: The Boots Co. Ltd. and Glaxo Group Ltd: A Report on the Proposed Mergers* (HC 341, 1972) pp. 49–51.
3. J. Jewkes, D. Sawers and R. Stillerman, *The Sources of Invention* (2nd ed., Macmillan, 1970).
4. H. G. Grabowski, 'The Determinants of Industrial Research and Development: A Study of the Chemical, Drug and Petroleum Industries', *Journal of Political Economy* (1968).
5. E. Mansfield, *Industrial Research and Technological Innovation* (Norton, 1968).
6. HC 341, *op. cit.*, p. 68.
7. W. Duncan Reekie, 'Location and Relative Efficiency of Research and Development in the Pharmaceutical Industry', *Business Ratios* (1969).
8. David Schwartzman, 'Research Activity and Size of Firm in the US Pharmaceutical Industry' (mimeographed, New School for Social Research, New York, 1973).

9. William S. Comanor, 'Research and Technical Change in the Pharmaceutical Industry', *Review of Economics and Statistics* (1965).
10. A. Angilley, 'Returns to Scale in Research in the Ethical Pharmaceutical Industry: Some Further Empirical Evidence', *Journal of Industrial Economics* (1973).
11. E. Mansfield, J. Rapaort, J. Schee, S. Wagner and M. Hamburger, *Research and Innovation in the Modern Corporation* (Norton, 1971).
12. J. E. S. Parker, 'Regulating Pharmaceutical Innovation: An Economist's View', *Food Drug Cosmetic Law Journal*, April (1977), p. 163.
13. *Ibid.*, p. 161.
14. William M. Wardell and Louis Lasagna, *Regulation and Drug Development* (American Enterprise Institute 1975), p. 122.
15. Grabowski (1976) *op. cit.*, p. 25.
16. Sam Peltzman, *Regulation of Pharmaceutical Innovation* (American Enterprise Institute, Washington, 1974).
17. Wardell and Lasagna, *op. cit.*
18. Rita Ricardo Campbell, *Drug Lag* (Houver Institution, Stanford University, 1976), p. 17.
19. *Ibid.*, p. 9.
20. *Ibid.*, p. 34.
21. *Ibid.*, p. 35.

NOTES TO CHAPTER 8

1. Conrad and Plotkin, *Risk and Rates of Return in US Industry* (Arthur D. Little, 1967).
2. Merret–Cyriax Associates, *Profitability in the Pharmaceutical Industry*, (London, 1968).
3. Sainsbury, *op. cit.*, pp. 40–41.
4. *Ibid.*, p. 53.
5. HC 197, *op. cit.*, para. 20.
6. Appendix to *Competition, Risk and Profit in the Pharmaceutical Industry* (Runnymede Research, 1975).
7. *Ibid.*, p. 46.
8. T. A. Lee, 'Enterprise Income, Survival or Decline and Fall', *Accounting and Business Research* (1974).
9. HC 197, *op. cit.*, para. 223.
10. Deferral of charging non-recurring R & D expenditures against profits was at least one contributory factor leading to the collapse of Rolls-Royce Ltd. in 1971.
11. Exposure Draft 17 proposed that, 'under certain circumstances' development expenditures be capitalised.
12. H. A. Clymer, 'The Changing Costs and Risks of Pharmaceutical Innovation', in J. Cooper (ed), *Economics of Innovation* (American University, 1970).
13. Ayanian, R., 'The Profit Rates and Economic Performance of Drug Firms', in Helms, *op. cit.*

14. T. Stauffer, 'Profitability Measures in the Pharmaceutical Industry', in Helms, *ibid.*
15. K. Clarkson, *Intangible Capital and Rates of Return* (Washington, D.C.: American Enterprise Institute for Public Policy Research, 1977).
16. *See* S. Peltzman, 'An Evalution of Consumer Protection Legislation: The 1962 Drug Amendments,' *Journal of Political Economy* (1973).
17. Schwartzman (1975) *op. cit.*, p. 36.
18. *Ibid.*, pp 40–41.

NOTE TO CHAPTER 9

1. Cooper (1977), *op. cit.*, pp 27–8.

Index